WHERE TOMORROWS AREN'T PROMISED

WHERE TOMORROWS AREN'T PROMISED

A MEMOIR

CARMELO ANTHONY
WITH D. WATKINS

GALLERY BOOKS

New York   London   Toronto   Sydney   New Delhi

G

Gallery Books
An Imprint of Simon & Schuster, Inc.
1230 Avenue of the Americas
New York, NY 10020

First Gallery Books hardcover edition September 2021

GALLERY BOOKS and colophon are registered trademarks of Simon & Schuster, Inc.

For information about special discounts for bulk purchases, please contact Simon & Schuster Special Sales at 1-866-506-1949 or business@simonandschuster.com.

The Simon & Schuster Speakers Bureau can bring authors to your live event. For more information or to book an event, contact the Simon & Schuster Speakers Bureau at 1-866-248-3049 or visit our website at www.simonspeakers.com.

Interior design by Erika R. Genova

Manufactured in the United States of America

10 9 8 7 6 5 4 3 2 1

Library of Congress Cataloging-in-Publication Data

Names: Anthony, Carmelo, 1984– author. | Watkins, D. (Dwight) other.
Title: Where tomorrows aren't promised : a memoir / Carmelo Anthony with D. Watkins.
Description: New York, N.Y. : Gallery Books, 2021. | Summary: "From iconic NBA All-Star Carmelo Anthony comes a raw and inspirational memoir about growing up in the housing projects of Red Hook and Baltimore–a brutal world Where Tomorrows Aren't Promised"— Provided by publisher.
Identifiers: LCCN 2021019923 (print) | LCCN 2021019924 (ebook) | ISBN 9781982160593 (hardcover) | ISBN 9781982160609 (trade paperback) | ISBN 9781982160616 (ebook)
Subjects: LCSH: Anthony, Carmelo, 1984– | Basketball players—United States—Biography
Classification: LCC GV884.A58 A3 2021 (print) | LCC GV884.A58 (ebook) | DDC 796.323092 [B]—dc23
LC record available at https://lccn.loc.gov/2021019923
LC ebook record available at https://lccn.loc.gov/2021019924

ISBN 978-1-9821-6059-3
ISBN 978-1-9821-6061-6 (ebook)

To every child who knows there is more to this life
than what people tell them is possible

NOTE TO READER

Some names in this book have been changed, and certain quotes have been reconstructed from memory.

WHERE
TOMORROWS
AREN'T
PROMISED

MADISON SQUARE GARDEN, NEW YORK, NEW YORK

D raft Night 2003: Flashing lights and the sounds of cameras clicking everywhere. The room was becoming more crowded. I moved to a different room, and the crowd followed as more people entered the venue. Everybody looked nervous but happy. Many of us would be experiencing meteoric social mobility, escaping a lifetime of poverty in a single night.

"Carmelo—over here, over here! Look this way, this way!" a group of photographers called out. From every non-ballplayer in the room, toting microphones and cameras, I'd heard over and over, again and again, "This is your big night." All the talking heads from ESPN, the same people I'd been watching for I don't know how long, were here in real life. They were pointing more microphones at me, at LeBron James, at Dwyane Wade, and at all of these other lanky prospects in tailored suits. *How did I get here?*

"What do you think is going to happen tonight?" interviewers asked me. "Where do you predict you will end up? Are you excited?"

Am I excited? I'm a Black kid from the bottom. I had to fight through some of the roughest housing projects in America. I'm standing here tonight as a potential top five, top three, maybe even top two NBA draft pick. *Am I excited?* I wished the cameras, reporters, and talking heads would just go away for a minute until I could regain my cool. It felt like my heart was making a fast break out of my suit.

I was excited, but I was also anxious and curious about what my new life was about to be. My mom had worked two jobs for as long as I could remember. Now I would be able take care of her, buy her a house, a car, a mink—whatever she wanted—and that was exciting. At the same time, I had mixed feelings, because my life had contained so many letdowns, bad endings, and traumas. I knew I had an agent, and I'd led the Syracuse Orange to their first-ever NCAA championship. I knew I'd won the Most Outstanding Player award. I was at the draft because I was invited and projected to go high. I was in this suit; however, none of these things guaranteed that these people were going to select me.

I would probably have been even more nervous and uncertain—except that my big brother Jus was there, and my big brother Wolf, and they always had my back. Regardless of what happened that night, I knew they would be there for me. I glanced over at them and looked at their feet. They were both were wearing slippery hard-bottoms, probably feeling as awkward as I did, because we never really wore suits. I bet that most of the athletes at this fancy event never wore suits, even though they were the reason for the event's existence.

My mom was there—my rock, the strongest woman I know—along with my heart, my big sister Michelle. When I'm anxious, their support and love settle me. If I could be in a position to give them everything they deserve, this whole journey would be worth it. I could be drafted by a team on Mars, and if my mom and Michelle agreed to come with me, then I'd go gladly. I'd know that everything was going to be okay. A lot of other families were in the room, and I imagined that the love I had for mine mirrored the love they shared. They probably waited their whole lives to celebrate this moment with family. I wondered if they felt like they belonged, or were they also haunted by old wounds?

Most basketball players dream of this night their whole lives—picking out their suits, memorizing their speeches, hoping and praying they didn't forget anyone. As kids, they probably rehearsed this moment by putting on little sport coats and the ball caps of their favorite teams, strutting across their living-room carpets, and pretending to shake hands with David Stern. They had it all mapped out, because the NBA was the goal, and every guy here made it happen. Dream fulfilled. The lights continued to flash, and the night progressed. LeBron was excited, Wade was excited. I was even excited for them, as well as for everybody at the Garden that night living their dreams. They were probably equally excited for me, thinking that I had achieved my dream, too. But what's funny is that the NBA wasn't my dream.

I'm not like most basketball players. I never obsessed over this day, this suit, or this moment of shaking David Stern's hand. Don't get me wrong, I was beyond grateful for these things. But until it actually happened, I just couldn't see it. I'm not sure if I didn't want to jinx myself or I thought it was too unreal, or if it was because for me, all of this top-player stuff just happened so fast. I just know I never thought about it. I never allowed myself to be lost in a dream that could be easily snatched away. So the appropriate question for me wasn't whether or not I was excited. The real question was, how did I—a kid who'd had so many hopes, dreams, and expectations beaten out of him—make it here at all?

RED HOOK, BROOKLYN

CHAPTER ONE

RED HOOK, BROOKLYN, 1989

"Lil' Curly! Come on, Chello, get off the court," they yelled at me. "Somebody catch him; he keeps fuckin' all the games up!"

I laughed as I zigzagged past all the older dudes on the blacktop in their jerseys, T-shirts with the sleeves ripped off, and multicolored Nikes and Adidas—highs and lows—across the concrete where I won my scrapes and bruises. Up over the curb and into my project building— my home. We lived in Red Hook West, apartment 1C, on the first floor of 79 Lorraine Street—the mecca of the neighborhood.

Apartment 1C was the spot, a hub made up of love, and everybody knew it. If you needed some food, some advice, or whatever, you could come to 1C. We were the most popular family inside our building and always had an influx of visitors from every end of the projects. Visitors were looking to hang around my siblings, eat all of my mom's cooking, or just connect with us, because that's the kind of family we were. My mom kept an open-door policy and never, ever, under any circumstances, turned anybody away. I can't imagine where Mom found the money needed to care for so many random people, but she made it work.

Apartment 1C was a huge three-bedroom unit. To me, it felt like a penthouse with unlimited space—even when seven people were living with us, or when our kitchen and living room were packed during holiday dinners, house parties, and any other family functions. Our spot never felt small and was more than enough space for everything I needed, including a place to sleep, eat, study, and blend in with the rotating mix of visiting residents who floated in and out of our unit. We had one of the most prominent families in Red Hook. At my crib, everybody—from killers and gangsters to kids and the elderly, and whoever else you can think of—touched our apartment one way or another. I welcomed them all to feast off our plates, drink out of our cups, and lounge in our living room. I loved our spot. My favorite part of our apartment was the side windows, which were two rectangular gateways to everything beyond my reach.

When I was too young to play outside by myself, I learned about the world through those windows. I heard stories, current affairs, jokes, and trauma. Everything spilled in by way of the people who posted up by those side windows. Their viewpoints and takes on society were more entertaining and informative than the shows on television. They fulfilled every need of my curious young mind. I had so many questions about where rain comes from, money, the neighborhood, the projects, cops, school, drugs, who makes the laws—and why we lived the way we did. All the answers came in through those windows.

At eye level, I just faced the sill. But after pushing our old speaker against the wall and climbing my small body on top of it, I could peer through the black iron bars. I could see hoopers, dreamers, rappers, and the rest of the older kids singing, dancing, and living life. The hustlers were in loud Pelle Pelle jackets trading dope for cash across from the girls yelling, playing jacks and double Dutch with ear-to-ear grins. Junkies were happy with their recent purchases and were itching to disappear into the shadows to turn up, while boys challenged each other to footraces. The cops loved breaking up happy crowds with their billy clubs and power trips. Little kids, just a little bigger than me, were scattered all over the playground where I always wanted to be. I couldn't wait to join them and mix in.

Some days, I'd watch my sister Michelle crush everybody in double Dutch. With ballerina footwork, she taught younger girls her moves. She held court with a crowd of people surrounding her, studying her, and hanging on her every word. I always wondered from a distance what she was talking about. It was probably the kind of information that I needed to know, survival skills mixed with the coolness she mastered and that made her such a draw. I'd watch my big brother Justice gambling with homies, knee-deep in a game of Cee-lo. He'd rattle three dice dizzy in his right hand, step back, pull up the bottoms of his jeans over his wheat-colored Timbs, and toss them against the graffiti-covered concrete wall. All the other guys around him waved their money in unison, howling in chorus. Opposite the dice games was the basketball court that my oldest brother, Big Wolf, owned. In-and-out crossover, heavy shoulder, post up, step-back, fadeaway, or whatever you wanted—Big Wolf had it in stock and was eager to serve you on that court. Nobody could check Wolf. In between some of Wolf's basketball games, the dudes from the court would run to the window for water, and I'd happily hand it to them. "Chello, put some ice in my cup, baby bro!" Sometimes Michelle and Justice would stop whatever they were doing to swing past the window to check on me, and I loved it, because they meant the world to me. Those three, directly and indirectly, provided the lessons on showing love, being humble, and remaining loyal, the lessons that guided me through my young life and that I still use to this very day.

There's a peculiar type of beauty that existed in Red Hook. Not necessarily in the architecture or layout of my projects but in how we Black and Brown people fit into and even accentuated the reality America apportioned to us. The racism, the poor schools, the crooked cops, the lack of positive outlets for young people, and the limited job opportunities for our parents—in combination with everything else holding us down—should have guaranteed our failure. Somehow, we still survived and sometimes even thrived.

It was easy for young me to absorb all the beauty my family and community offered, despite the chaos in my neighborhood. However, I was never naive about the environment surrounding my building. I saw people throwing blows on the basketball court over a bad call, dudes whipping guns out, and people robbing each other. In the midst of all this, we would sit on the stoop together, taking it all in. We supported victims whenever we could, and we watched how we moved as a family— because that was Red Hook, too. A place where danger was tangled up with beauty, and you couldn't untie one from the other.

CHAPTER TWO

A BRIEF HISTORY OF RED HOOK

If you walked through my neighborhood, you would see a collection of large brick buildings inhabited by nothing but Black and Brown faces. I knew there were other types of people in New York. It's the most diverse city racially, ethnically, and culturally in the country. Yet in my neighborhood, everybody had the same skin color as me or some variation of it—and I always wondered why this was so, even at the age of five. I have always done this. I see things, conjure up questions inside my head, and become fixated, wondering why things are the way they are. At a young age, I relied on Jus, Michelle, and my mom for most of my answers. Wolf, too, when he was around. When I got older, I got into books and history, and I learned how to do my own digging. I wanted to figure out, why do Black and Brown people all live together? Who put us in Red Hook, who put us in the projects, where were all the white people, and why is it like this?

I learned that my neighborhood was founded by the Dutch in the seventeenth century. My section of Brooklyn earned its name, "Roode Hoek," meaning "red point," from its red clay soil and hooklike shape that resembles a curved finger on any map of BK. The land that makes up Red Hook extends from the coast of Brooklyn and is surrounded by the water of the Upper New York Bay on three sides.

From the mid-1800s to well into the 1900s, Red Hook's proximity to water created a thriving industrial neighborhood. Italian and Irish dock-workers fought for their piece of the American dream, meaning money and land. These immigrants saw Red Hook as a place to unite and keep alive the traditions from their origin countries while still offering them everything New York had to offer.

On June 22, 1944, President Franklin D. Roosevelt, FDR, signed the Servicemen's Readjustment Act. Better known as the G.I. Bill, it was part of his New Deal reforms intended to deliver America from the Great Depression and support veterans returning home from World War II. The bill set up hospitals, offered low-interest mortgages with no down-payment requirements, and provided for tuition and expenses for veterans who wanted to attend college. From 1944 to 1949, nearly 9 million veterans received an estimated $4 billion from the bill's unemployment program.

Black veterans thought they were coming home to receive those same benefits. They, too, had left their families and fought alongside white soldiers to protect America during World War II. I imagine they dreamed of reuniting with their families, buying land, building beautiful homes, and obtaining a higher education. Remember, these men were only a generation or so removed from slavery. If they were from the South, their parents were most likely sharecroppers, and their grandparents had been enslaved people, so this war allowed them to hope. This would be their first crack at a real opportunity toward that American dream our country sells so well—to own property and experience upward social mobility. But after the war ended, the ugly storm of racism washed away all those hopes and dreams.

Many African Americans were denied the very tuition money they had fought for and had been promised. The lucky ones who received that so-called guaranteed money for college didn't have many schools to choose from, due to segregation. We saw the same thing happen with housing. Banks denied African American veterans their guaranteed loans because of skin color, so they were never able to build those dream homes for their families. White people took all of that G.I. Bill money and used it as the seeds that grew the suburbs. This established white generational wealth while Blacks were left to fend for themselves in

America's big cities. So what did FDR offer Black people in his historic New Deal? Simple: the projects.

Alfred Easton Poor was a big-time architect from Baltimore, Maryland. He was known for several private and federal projects, including the Jacob K. Javits Federal Building, the James Madison Memorial Building, and the Wright Brothers National Memorial. Poor designed the forty-acre Red Hook Houses back in 1939. This was a few years before the G.I. Bill was signed but still under the same Roosevelt administration. Our projects were made up of two conjoining buildings, Red Hook East and Red Hook West, making it the largest housing complex in Brooklyn. Red Hook East had sixteen residential buildings and three nonresidential buildings. Red Hook West, where my home was located, added fourteen residential buildings and one nonresidential structure. Featuring concrete playgrounds and tattered blacktops with net-less rims, it was almost like they were grooming us to play ball.

Now, initially, there had been Irish and Italian families throughout Red Hook. By the 1960s, container shipping had begun to replace bulk shipping, and many of the businesses in and around Red Hook's ports moved to New Jersey. Unemployment spread like a disease, and the neighborhood fell into a state of decline. This gave a criminal element the opportunity to develop quickly.

As Blacks and Puerto Ricans started filling the projects, many Irish and Italian families fled. The remaining Italian and Irish families established neighborhoods in a predominantly white section, which we called the "Back" of Red Hook. I was taught that those communities hated Black people, and I knew to stay well away from there. "Never go to the Back, it's crazy racist out there!" my brother Jus would always say. It seemed like there was always something terrible happening to Black and Puerto Rican people who mixed in with those white neighborhoods. Countless stories of race-fueled crimes terrorized my childhood, but the story of Kevin Teague from 1997 always stuck out the most. I heard it told over and over again. Teague was a Black postal worker who was minding his business and getting off the subway. While heading home, he was beaten nearly to death by four racist white men who had gotten into an argument at a McDonald's with another group of Black men Teague didn't even know. Teague needed thirteen stitches to close his wounds. He suffered severe damage to his eye and was struck by the car of one of the assailants. Despite these facts, Justice Alan D. Marrus of the State Supreme Court in Brooklyn found his attackers—Anthony Mascuzzio, Ralph Mazzatto, and Alfonse and Andrew Russo—not guilty of what was clearly an attempted murder and a hate crime. That's the system in a nutshell if you were Black and from Red Hook. These stories added weight to my brother's warnings to stay away from those neighborhoods. The Back of Red Hook had a reputation for being racist long before I was born, and unfortunately, it remains so to this day. What's worse is that the system, as Judge Marrus represented perfectly, proudly cosigns these racist actions. If you are nonwhite and live in a place like Red Hook, you'd better be prepared to deal with one-sided justice.

When I came into the world on May 29, 1984, Red Hook was still in deep economic decline, with little to no opportunities for its Black residents. By 1988, the violence in Brooklyn regularly captured national attention. *Life* magazine even ran a nine-page cover story on my neighborhood, branding it "the crack capital of America." I didn't know anything about any of that stuff or the world I was being born into. My mother told everybody that I was going to be her last child, and my siblings were so excited to be getting a brand-new baby brother.

CHAPTER THREE

THE FAMILY

My dad died of cancer when I was two years old. Because of this fact, I don't have a mental library of Disney-movie-like fishing-trip memories. No stories about the day he took the training wheels off my bike and watched me soar down Lorraine Street. No lessons from him on dealing with the madness that comes with being Black, Puerto Rican, or both in America.

He did leave me a small gold chain with a Jesus piece, though. I cherished it and rocked it daily, never tucking it inside my shirt. I proudly wore it wherever I went, because it was the only piece I had of a father I never really knew. That necklace connected us, and my mom always told me, "Do not let anyone touch it!" She knew its personal value would only accumulate as I grew older. I listened to her, for the most part. Then one day, my close friend Tyree said, "Yo, Curly, can I hold your chain?"

"Nah, man," I said. "I'm really not supposed to let anybody touch this necklace. It came from my dad."

"Come on, yo, don't be stingy, man, it's me. I'll give it right back!"

My mom had meant strangers, but this was my best friend. Tyree and I played every day: hide and go seek, tag, and basketball. Letting him hold it would be okay. Against my instinct, which was probably a direct message from my dad up above, I unlatched the necklace and placed it in his hand as he grinned. He wrapped it around his neck, fastened the clasp, adjusted it over his shirt, and posed. I nodded my head in approval, because I didn't realize that I'd never see that necklace again. A week later, I saw him and noticed that he wasn't wearing it anymore. I pressed him. "Yo, where is my necklace?" He faked like he was looking for it and had misplaced it, scratching his head, looking up at the clouds, saying, "I'll get it to you tomorrow." But I knew he had stolen it, and tomorrow was never coming. I never caught him wearing it after that, but I knew he had it and was hiding it from me. Even knowing how important it was to me, my best friend stole my most prized possession. My mom could punish me, but she couldn't possibly make me feel any worse. That had been from my dad, my only piece of him. Other than a few faded photos and some stories from the streets, that necklace was the only thing that proved my dad had ever lived at all. Now it was gone, just like him.

My dad's government name was Carmelo Iriarte. Everybody from the neighborhood called him Curly because he wore a big afro with long, dark curls. As a baby, I looked just like him—same hair and all—which is why they used to call me Lil' Curly. Pops was born in Puerto Rico and moved to New York when he was young. In his early years, he developed a love for poetry and documented it in a huge binder that he carried with him everywhere, just in case he was inspired and needed to capture his feelings.

Curly's work ethic in everything he did was legendary; everyone who knew him back in Red Hook always told me about how much of a "go-getter" he was. He had a reputation for being a great basketball player, and that "go-getter" mentality had him running down loose balls and applying extra pressure on defense. If my dad wanted something, he applied himself and found a way to have it—on the court, in the community, and on the jobs he worked.

My dad's main job for over twenty years was at the post office across the street from Madison Square Garden. Curly always used the money he made at work to take care of everybody back in Red Hook. If you were short on cash, Curly had your back. Whenever or wherever, it didn't matter—if someone needed Curly, he was there. From helping older women cross the street to buying families groceries from the bodega when they needed it, the streets said Curly was always pulling up for his friends.

He took care of his own in the streets as well. When they had a beef with outsiders, he was the first on the front line, ready to fight, holding his big fists high like prizes. He loved his people and was excited to protect them. Curly was never afraid to stand up for them or for what he believed. I imagine my father's commitment to the people originated with and was nurtured by his days as a Young Lord in New York.

The Young Lords was a civil rights organization that was heavily influenced by the Black Panthers. They fought for social programs, including the free school breakfast for children that still runs today, better healthcare, and improved overall quality of life for working-class Latinos. The New York chapter of the Young Lords was founded and led by educated Latinos trained in leftist theory. Just like the Panthers, they mastered a language that attracted young street people to their righteous cause, which attracted a guy like Curly—smart enough to understand the ideas, tough enough to put in the work.

Some say my pops had the biggest heart in Red Hook, maybe all of Brooklyn. This alone would have made him a natural standout, but it didn't hurt that he also stood six foot six and sported a huge Puerto Rican 'fro. Had he survived, I know he would've been more than a hero to me in my formative years. He would've taught me how to square up just like him, to use my fist to guard my face while bobbing and weaving in battle. He would've made sure I protected my friends, the same way he always looked out for his. Pops would've shown me how to tie my Nikes tight enough to pop the laces, pull my shorts up, slap the court with both hands, and strap down on D during basketball games. Getting the block or the steal, running the break, hitting a spin move, dropping the ball in for an easy bucket. And Pops would have given me a smooth line or two to use when I pressed up on girls from the neighborhood. I imagine the combination of Curly's talent, charm, wit, and popularity is what made my mom fall in love with him.

My mother, Mary Anthony, moved to New York against her wishes when she was eighteen. Employment opportunity in the south was slow and she headed to the city with her mom in search of more opportunity. Her family was originally from a small town in South Carolina. There she had been a basketball star like her father, who was also her best friend. You could say hooping is in every part of my DNA. Many people from the South fantasized about that New York big-city life—the clubs, the tall buildings, the action, and the adventure. She, however, wasn't impressed by any of that. Mom was her own person, and she has always followed her own path. She dreamed of building a successful but modest life in the South. She also realized that hard work was necessary to accomplish that goal, regardless of where she lived. Once my mother found out she had to move with her mom to New York, she didn't complain. She just figured that she could make it work. So Mom packed her bags, as well as her sweet smile and Southern ambition, and moved to Brooklyn.

Life experience taught my mother that having your own meant freedom. Relying on others was the exact opposite—and it was no way to live. That mentality served her well in New York, and she always pushed my older siblings toward independence. To this day, I can still see her standing tall in front of the TV. Every Saturday, we watched countless hours of kung fu flicks, and she'd be there waving her finger and instructing me not to depend on anyone else to do for me. She always told me to reach for the stars even if they seemed unattainable. She taught me never to settle for less, and I listened.

Mom also stressed the importance of education. As beautiful as many of the residents in our Red Hook community were, some people got dragged down by the lack of opportunities society had to offer them. They carried a pain that made them appear as though they had never experienced love. My mother didn't want me to have any part of that sad reality—the inability to put bread on the table, have a stable home, and take care of yourself in general.

My mom always did her job. Brown, strong, regal, yet still soft and always offering a huge smile. She was the best mother in Red Hook, hands down, and I'm not just saying this because she's my mother. Because of this fact, at times, Red Hook needed her to be everybody's mother. She took care of our whole family, she allowed relatives to live with us when they fell on hard times, and she managed all our struggles while making it look easy. She kept me in all kinds of programs and extracurricular activities. She also exposed my siblings and me to things that many of the other children in Red Hook didn't get a chance to experience, like art and life outside the neighborhood. My favorite was the long train rides into the city where we'd go to the American Museum of Natural History or The Metropolitan Museum of Art, where I'd spend hours looking at the large beautiful paintings.

I loved wrestling—the over-the-top personalities that matched the cracked story lines, the wild colorful costumes, the drama, the screaming, the body slams, the downfalls, the comebacks, the show! I'd rearrange the bunk beds in my room, turning them into a makeshift ring, then fly off the top right onto one of my brothers' or cousins' heads. Mom laughed at me running around the apartment like Ric Flair, screaming "WOOOOOOOOOOOOOO!" She started taking me to all the WWF matches at the Garden. There I saw Hulk Hogan ripping off his shirt in anticipation of battle and the Undertaker ready to bury anyone. I saw the Ultimate Warrior and Randy "Macho Man" Savage exciting the crowd. I loved it when Bret "The Hitman" Hart would run up and down the aisle, making everybody go crazy. And at one point, Mom started loving wrestling more than I did.

We also went to the movies regularly as a family—Mom, Big Wolf, Justice, Michelle, and me. During the long train rides back to our building, we loved to discuss what we'd seen. Mom also enjoyed taking us on picnics, which was rare for people from my part of Brooklyn. When the weather broke, my mom packed her tote. We headed out to set up in the shade at Prospect Park, Coney Island, Highland Park, or Central Park. We would eat chicken, potato, macaroni, and green salads that went perfectly with the hamburgers and hot dogs she'd throw on the grill. My mother could whip up anything on the grill or in the kitchen or wherever.

And people knew this, which was why we had a different cast of charac-
ters eating at our house almost every night. They'd smell the aroma waft-
ing around our door and knock, asking, "Hey, Miss Mary, you got room
for one more?" What's even more impressive is that she did all of this
entertaining, teaching, laughing, dancing, hosting, cooking, cleaning,
and living while holding two jobs, working at the school and at the bank.

Early on, things were tough for my mom, same as they were for most
Black women raising small kids in public housing. Still, she couldn't
see herself relying on social service, especially since that organization
didn't help to advance families out of the system. So she recruited one
of her friends in the building to watch us at night while she went to
school. Mom attended night school and earned a certificate in business
reception. But that wasn't good enough for her, so she went to business
secretary school, completed the course, and quickly graduated.

Her first postgraduation job was as a receptionist at an ex-offender
program on Smith Street in Brooklyn. There she met with newly released
citizens, prepared them for interviews, and helped them find jobs. Many
formerly incarcerated individuals would come into the office confused
and intimidated. Regardless of their past, my mother treated them with
the respect all people deserve, and she made sure they had what they
needed to join the workforce. She always believed that people shouldn't
be judged by their worst mistakes and that everybody deserves a second
chance. Mom stayed there for about two years, then started working at
Urban Trust Bank in Manhattan. Eventually, she landed at Chase Manhattan Bank as a secretary.

Through our ups and downs, Mom also always relied on God. She
loved Jesus, lived by his words, and was a deaconess at our neighborhood
church. Now, I wasn't one of those kids who clung to religion, but Mom
did work really hard at teaching me how to see what she saw. I was too
young to understand, but I respected it because I respected her.

Mom took me to church and Bible study a couple of times. Sometimes my cousin Omar would come along as well. Mom would park the
two of us right in the front pew—courtside. We were close enough to see

the sweat on the preacher's forehead in the midst of all his antics. Now, most people don't really know what a deacon or deaconess does, so I'll tell you: they are the people who are solely responsible for holding the church together. This could include anything from plumbing to organizing a bake sale, from managing the church's money to directing traffic on a busy Sunday, from DJ-ing the Easter kiddie disco to teaching karate to the congregation—if it is to be done, deacons and deaconesses do it.

One Sunday, Mom was up there speaking, doing her thing as a deaconess. When she finished, the pastor made his way over to the pulpit and started preaching, singing, performing—really working the crowd. As the pastor launched a tirade against the devil, people in the church started singing Jesus's praises, screaming up to God, and crying. The organist pounded the keys, adding a crescendo of accompaniment to the clamor that filled the church. One lady, who must have been a member, because she sat in the same row as us, suddenly leaped up higher than Michael Jordan. She slid across the front of the church like Michael Jackson.

"Yo yo!" I laughed to Omar. "She really rockin'! She rockin' off! Look at her go!"

"What's that dance called?" Omar laughed back. "I gotta learn it, cuz!"

I didn't know what was going on, but she kept floating up and down the aisle. Apparently, this was the Holy Ghost or what's called "Catching the Holy Spirit and getting happy with the Lord." I had never seen that before or understood what it was. I saw *The Color Purple*, but I hadn't really understood that movie when I was younger. Neither had Omar, so we were laughing, in tears, and pointing, while the older church members frowned, looking at us like we stole money from them. We didn't care, we kept hitting each other. "Yo, look! Look, she rockin'! She rockin' off!"

My mom stood at the side bench, giving that look only an angry Black mother can give. Our laughing stopped instantly. I knew she was mad, because she didn't let me go to Bible study after. In fact, she took us straight home, yelling at us the whole way—"Don't you play with the

Lord" and all of that. I didn't fully understand her anger at the time, but Mom had made herself clear. I never joked about religion around her ever again. That was one of the few times I made my mom really upset; other than that, I was a good kid who followed the rules. Mostly, we just had fun.

We didn't travel out of the state or to other countries. We didn't do wild, extravagant things over the summer. But I never felt the need for any of that stuff. My mom worked hard and never hesitated to make those trips to the city parks. She made Rye Playland in Upstate New York feel like trips to Disney World. Everything was always fun, and we stayed wrapped up in the joy of each other's company.

Hands down, Mary Anthony was the best mother in Red Hook.

CHAPTER FOUR

THE LIVEST UNIT IN RED HOOK

My home was live. It was a twenty-four-hour reality television show, full of love, drama, and all of the craziness that comes with a bunch of people living under one roof.

We had the first apartment on the left, right by the elevator, as soon as you entered the six-story complex. So we caught all of the action our building had to offer, from kissing teens sneaking in late at night, to fighting couples cursing each other out, to curious new residents surveying the lay of the land, to older residents being shipped out. We saw it all, and we saw it first.

At times, we fit up to ten people into our three-bedroom apartment. My mom had four children but was willing to take in any kids from our extended family who needed help. This included my big cousin Luck, who slid by for a visit one day and ended up becoming a resident. Regardless of whether we had space or finances to spare, my mom would make sure everyone was okay. She was going to open our doors, and we were going to make it work.

Mom and my stepdad Deek had the room in the back. It was off-limits, and none of us kids went back there. My older sister Michelle's room was next to theirs.

Michelle was the rock of the family. She held everything down for all of us boys and basically raised me while my mom was at work. Her presence meant the world to me, because she was a real neighborhood superstar, the first superstar who loved me. From the good girls to the baddest girls, from the hustlers, money chasers, pistol grippers, and gun slangers to the old heads and little kids, everybody checked for, wanted to be around, and just had to connect with her at all times. My sister was a natural storyteller. She was linguistically gifted and had a unique way of breaking things down to me on a personal tip. Seeing her twirl the neighborhood around her little finger using her legendary charm and wit was magical. Michelle was the Mary J. Blige of Red Hook, even before Mary was a star. Michelle was beautiful, she could fight, and she rocked the flyest everything. She always had a ton of people flocking around her, listening, soaking up game, and living off her energy. Her crew was all little versions of her, girls who were loyal and would do anything to make Michelle happy.

We boys shared the room next to Michelle's. Our bunk beds were arranged perfectly to fit me, my big brothers Wolf and Justice, and my cousin Luck. Wolf is the oldest brother, and dude was always a mystery to me, and I mean that in the most loving way possible. Wolf would just get lost—not literally, but he would just go his own way, deep into his own world. I remember when we were out looking for him around the holidays one year. We weren't scared or bugged out, because this was how Wolf moved, and finding him was always an adventure. We started in Red Hook first, then shot over to my aunt's place in Queens, and checked with family in Fort Greene, over by the Farragut Houses. Wolf could be anywhere in Brooklyn, but he was in Bed-Stuy mostly, which is near Fort Greene. However, this was Wolf, so it wouldn't be too strange to see him walking out of Yankee Stadium or down with the Wall Street stockbrokers in Manhattan or courtside at a Knicks game. Wolf was just that kind of guy, and looking for him didn't necessarily mean we were going to find him—he's been like that forever.

My mom really wanted to check on him this time, so we continued to comb New York, driving through every section of Queens and Brooklyn. We'd spot familiar faces and ask, "Did you guys see Wolf?" Some people said they seen him over here, seen him over there, or we had just missed him. The blocks in New York are just endless, but we kept driving, and we randomly saw him bopping around the corner—mellow, cool, and laid-back.

"Yo, where you comin' from?" I said, laughing.

Wolf looked around. He was always discreet and never, under any circumstances, gave a straight answer or explained himself.

"Don't worry about it. I'm good. I'm good, I'm good," he said, "Y'all good?"

Wolf would be here today, gone tomorrow, and then strangely pop up again. Just when you got used to him being gone, you'd see his tall frame making its way across the basketball court. In his absence, I'd always hear so many stories about how great a ballplayer he was. As people watched me run up and down the playground with my friends, playing full-court and learning the game, they'd say, "Nobody in Red Hook can touch Wolf. He could be the best in New York!" As far as basketball went, I wanted to be just like my big brother. Whether I was checking rock by the monkey bars or hanging a wire hanger on the back of the bedroom door and dunking it with a taped-up sock, I wasn't emulating an NBA player, I was emulating Wolf.

My brother Justice is the opposite of Wolf. They both ran the streets, but Justice was always into strategy, ideas, and knowledge. It didn't matter if we were laughing, joking, or in the middle of a heated argument. Justice was always dropping gems, telling stories, and leaving me with lessons to live by. Justice's reputation was solid everywhere. He never had to talk about himself, brag about his work, or personally define his character. Everyone else did it for him. He's just an exceptionally impressive dude with an unexplainable light that has always guided me. Even when the streets intertwined with Justice's personality, a divine energy blessed his path.

One day, he was walking home from the video store after renting some tapes. Justice turned the corner onto our block and made his way toward the courtyard in front of our home. Two big-time drug dealers were banging it out over territory, firing shots that could be heard clear across the projects. People ran, screamed, ducked, and hid behind cars and near the playground, taking cover. One of the shooters noticed young Justice standing there watching and yelled, "Ayoooo! Put the guns down! Stop shooting until lil' man gets in the building!" They stopped. Justice eyed both of the shooters, gave them a nod, and made his way into the house to embrace our mom, who watched the whole thing through the window. Then the gunshots resumed. Justice didn't blindly follow behind people. He questioned everything and passed that same mentality down to Luck and me.

Drama, pain, and uncertainty were going on at Luck's house, so he came to live with us. Younger than Justice but older than me, Luck was able to bridge the gap between all of us boys. He became more of a brother than a cousin. I was excited when he moved in, even though we had to share a bed. With Luck there, I had somebody to ride my bike with, play basketball with, make me tougher, and challenge me on everything in a way that made me smarter. Most important, Luck could translate what was happening in and around Red Hook into a language that I could understand, taking his time to point out what was good and what was bad. He taught me to watch for guys who wore masks, or people begging for change, or unfamiliar cars on the block. Luck never said these things would be dangerous, but he gave me the ability to be hyper-aware, so that I would not end up in a bad situation. His rules forced me to become wise beyond my years and made me into one of the most awake and alert little dudes to ever come through those projects.

CHAPTER FIVE

A WAY OUT

"The principal of a grade school in one of Brooklyn's toughest neighborhoods, a dedicated, gentle man who often took children by the hand through streets ruled by violence, was shot and killed yesterday as he searched for a missing pupil in a crime-ridden housing project" (*New York Times*, December 18, 1992).

His name was Patrick Daily, and that "crime-ridden housing project" was my home. Daily was the principal of Public School 15 over on 71 Sullivan Street. Dude loved his job, but he loved his students even more. That day, he was in our projects checking on a fourth-grader who had left school early because of a fight. On local TV and in all of our newspapers, Daily had documented the struggles with violence in our community and his mission to create a safe and positive learning environment for his students. So it wasn't strange to see him all up in, around, and through the projects talking to students, checking on their parents, and trying to strengthen his school. Daily was well aware of the risks of being in Red Hook Houses, but nobody thought something like this would happen. As the streets say, "Bullets don't have a name." The principal was caught in the crossfire between two hustlers banging it out in broad daylight, and a single shot ripped through Daily's chest. He was only forty-eight years old. His last words were "Thank you."

Our neighborhood reportedly had twenty murders, ten rapes, 526 robberies, and 364 assaults the year before Principal Daily lost his life.

So imagine the number of unreported crimes that went down. Pistols banged all day and night—it felt like our apartment was in the middle of a gun range. The sound of discharging firearms had become as routine as hail in January. It was so common that at times, I'd turn up the television to muffle the noise. The shootouts were always about drug business, drug beef, drug connections, or otherwise drug-related—or so I was told. So many young people from the neighborhood were locked out of the workforce. This seemed to be for unfair reasons, like racism or lack of job opportunities. However, the dope slingers were always hiring, and they never discriminated. That created the reality of too many hungry people fighting for territory, sales, and power, and there was no shortage of guns. If we were at the height of the war on drugs, then drugs were clearly winning. And we—the Black and Brown residents of the city—were losing.

Sick of the violence, sick of the killings, sick of the drugs, and sick of all the negativity plaguing our neighborhood, my mother was officially done with New York. She was ready to move back down South. Michelle was already grown, Wolf was fully committed to the streets, and Justice was running wild. So it was just her and me and Luck.

Justice was never into basketball as much as Wolf and I were, but he'd play pickup and street games from time to time. Coney Island projects had challenged the kids from Red Hook for money, so Justice and some of his homies traveled to their side of Brooklyn. They arrived to find out the game was canceled. Justice was upset that he had wasted his time. The entire Red Hook squad was made up of hustlers, so he figured they could've stayed around the neighborhood, made some money, or done something more useful than traveling all the way to Coney Island for nothing.

"Yo, Jus, what up?" a guy yelled from the other side of the basketball court. Justice squinted his eyes and saw it was Sherrod. This dude had gone to school with him, but now he was living in Coney Island and on the run from another part of Brooklyn.

"I know y'all mad, y'all came alla way out here," Sherrod said. "That guy King crazy for canceling the game on some clown shit. That nigga think he can do what he want cuz he slangin' all that dope out here in Coney Island."

"Oh, word?" Justice replied.

"Yeah, all those dudes over there are like his little lieutenants," Sherrod continued. "They getting to it. I be seeing them have fiends wrapped around the block, waitin'. You know I got the green light on them kids, too. I been watchin' them for months."

It didn't take much for Justice to read between the lines. Sherrod had a target, some solid information, and he was looking for muscle.

"Come back up here tonight if you wanna roll. I'll beep you, I got y'all," Sherrod said.

Justice and his friends returned to Red Hook to continue their day. Sherrod kept his word and paged him that night. So Justice strapped up, grabbed his Champion hoodie, and recruited his man Black. They hopped into a gypsy cab and headed all the way back out to Coney Island. When they arrived, Justice spotted some of the guys Sherrod had identified as lieutenants still hanging in the park.

"That's them right there," Justice told Black. The two slowly approached them.

"Kick all that shit out!" Immediately, one of the Coney Island kids grabbed Black. Justice aimed his pistol, licking off two shots. "POP! POP!" But they didn't hit anyone. Some white boys in the deli across the street heard the shots and saw Justice and Black breaking away from the tussle and running across the park. I imagine they were suspicious of the duo because Justice was wearing a hoodie in the summertime—so the white boys dropped their sandwiches or whatever they were buying and started chasing them.

Justice and Black continued running, picking up pace, weaving in between cars, cutting through alleys, and exploding onto the block while dumping their hoodies and masks. The white boys caught up, recognizing Black and Justice from the park.

"Freeze!" one of them yelled, as another pulled his weapon and banged off two shots in Justice's direction. The bullets blew past him, bouncing off the wall and a car. Black continued running to the other side of the street, taking cover and shooting back.

"Yo, I think they cops!" Justice yelled to Black.

"Fuck that, nigga, just blast!" Black shouted back.

Justice emptied the clip in their direction and continued down the block. As the white boys continued pursuing, Justice broke his gun into pieces and started throwing them in different directions. Black headed another way. When the coast was clear, Justice dove into a patch of grass.

"Stop, police!" the officers yelled, pulling in from a different direction.

He was caught. Game over. A simple trip to play basketball for money had turned into a shootout with NYPD, and now Justice was facing some serious time in prison.

Deek was just as fed up as my mom was with everything that was going on in Red Hook, so he wanted to go back to South Carolina. However, my mom wanted to stay closer to New York to be near Wolf and to support Justice as he faced legal trouble. So Baltimore, which wasn't too far north or too far south, was the compromise. We had family there, and it was cheaper than New York—plus, if Wolf or Justice needed my mom, she could get to them quickly. It was also easy to get farther down South by bus or train from Baltimore.

I was only eight years old, so I didn't have a say in staying or leaving, but I wanted to stay. I loved Red Hook—the playground, my friends, my brothers, and all of the extended family we'd grown to love. From the people who hung around our window with jokes and stories to the random visitors who smelled my mom's cooking in the hallway and popped over for dinner every night, they all would be missed.

Moving to Baltimore meant losing everything. Baltimore meant that I'd never enjoy the Paradise Classic ever again. The Paradise Classic was the best day in Red Hook, when everybody came out, and we all partied, played music, and grilled food, and the basketball tournaments went on all day. And as soon as I'd leave the court after the tournaments, the rest of my friends were waiting to play tag until it was time to eat. Then we'd devour the hot dogs and hamburgers coming fresh off the grill and wash them down with sugary red punch. Afterward, we'd lock our scrawny arms together and play Red Rover. And I'd grin ear to ear when my turn came around, and everybody would yell, "Red Rover! Red Rover! Send Curly right over!" I'd blast through the line of the other team, breaking their chain of linked arms every time.

I knew there was nothing like the Paradise Classic in Baltimore. I knew I would have to make new friends, and I would have to do it without Wolf and Justice. It was going to be strange pedaling my bike through a new neighborhood without people stopping me and saying, "You Justice's lil' brother, right?" or "Isn't Michelle ya sista? Hey, Lil' Curly! What's up?"

We'd be making a fresh start. I wouldn't have my big brothers around, but I did have my mom's love. Michelle was coming to Baltimore, which was a blessing, along with Luck, with whom I had been spending most of my time.

Watching Luck play basketball had made me care even more about the game. I also noticed his style, the way he wore his boots with the laces undone, twisted his Yankees fitted hat to the side. I noted the respect he got from some of the older dudes, always giving him half-hugs and pounds like "What's up, Lucky!" Luck was the blueprint of what I was trying to be. My stepdad was old. He always had his rusty toolbox, and sore arms and sore shoulders from working all the time. He didn't know what was going on in the streets—he probably couldn't tell the difference between some shell-head Adidas and a pair of Air Jordans. My big brothers were out conquering the world, so even though they looked out when they could, they didn't have time to school me. Michelle was a woman, and even though she was slicker than most, some things women just can't teach us men, and vice versa. So I needed somebody—a male, in my generation—to guide me. I never asked Luck to show me how the streets worked, he just did it. I also don't think Luck saw it as his responsibility, it just came naturally to him. He was a natural leader. Luck's moves had groomed me to survive Red Hook; they would also prepare me for Baltimore.

I didn't want to leave Red Hook. But together, Luck and I were going to make Baltimore work.

BALTIMORE

CHAPTER SIX

A NEW CITY

The ride from Red Hook to Baltimore is about three and a half hours. People always say it's two hours and forty-five minutes, but that's only if you pretend traffic doesn't exist—which it does. The borough of Manhattan and the packed New Jersey Turnpike and 95 South are all jammed with traffic. The journey south felt long, but there was so much on the other side of the window for me to see—Red Hook projects getting smaller and smaller and disappearing in the side mirror as we pulled away, the fleet of endless yellow cabs that flooded Manhattan, families like mine packed into cars headed south on 95, the buildings and rest stops and more buildings as we drove, venturing over hours of road, heading toward that sign reading *Welcome to Baltimore*.

Baltimore is one of the few major cities in America that maintains that small-town feel. Its population always floats around 600,000 residents, but it feels like everybody knows everybody. The town was founded in 1729 and named after Englishman Cecil Calvert, Lord Baltimore. In the years that followed, the Germans and Scots settled on the cheap land. The soil was too poor for tobacco farming, which was what most planters in Maryland at the time relied on. But that same land was perfect for growing wheat. Proximity to water helped Baltimore flourish and establish a thriving ship market at Fell's Point, which went on to become a popular area full of bars, restaurants, and expensive homes. They sold slaves there as well.

Baltimore blew up in a major way. As industry grew, so did the need for slaves, hence the slave auction that was held right in the center of Fell's. By 1810, Baltimore had 4,672 slaves, the majority hired out by cash-strapped owners from upper Maryland. The most notable of these was Frederick Douglass, who traveled down to Baltimore and made money before he became the nation's most popular abolitionist. In the heyday of the antebellum South, before the Civil War, some of those Baltimore slaves made enough money on the side to buy their own freedom and eventually the freedom of their families and friends. Hustling to make money is something that Baltimoreans always took pride in. At one point, Baltimore had the largest freed Black population in the country.

Even though it was a slave state, Maryland sided with the Union during the Civil War by not declaring secession. Still, some people in southern Maryland joined the Confederates anyway in an attempt to keep their slaves and their tobacco farms. Some Confederate supporters attacked Union soldiers, causing twelve deaths and the Baltimore riot of 1861. After that, the Union Army had to step in and occupy Baltimore until 1865. That is why there have always been two Baltimores. It's a city split on ideologies, because it's too South to be North and too North to be South. Coming from New York, my entire family looked at Baltimore as being country and full of Southern culture. Later we came to understand that the people saw themselves as being more Northern. Either way, here we were in our new city. It was full of new people moving, shaking, and running in every direction. I watched them all from the passenger-side window of our truck until we finally arrived on our new block, in front of our new home at 1122 Myrtle Avenue.

Our block was made up of modest row houses that sat between Dolphin and Hoffman Streets. We parked in the middle of the block, staring directly at a group of buildings they called Murphy Homes. These structures dominated the end of our street, beginning on Hoffman at the corner of Myrtle and stretching across an eternity of grass, concrete, and cement. Now, technically, I did not live in Murphy Homes; however, that is where I'm from, where I spent most of my time, and the place I learned the majority of the valuable lessons I live by today, but I'll get to that.

We had the red row house. It was the only home on the block painted that color.

"We're home!" Mom said. "We are home!"

I surveyed the block. In New York, everything had been apartments and tall buildings, but this was a house. At the same time, it was adjacent to the famous George B. Murphy Homes, Baltimore's biggest public housing complex. Murphy Homes was named after George B. Murphy Sr., one of the founders of Baltimore's Afro-American newspapers and the patriarch of an elite Black family. It was full of lawyers, judges, doctors, and politicians, none of whom probably ever stepped foot in, let alone lived in, this neighborhood. The projects sat on about fifteen acres. The landscape consisted of red brick low-rise town houses, playgrounds, and basketball courts, wrapped around four fourteen-story red brick high-rises or towers full of one-, two-, and three-bedroom apartments. I'd had a few experiences of being in Murphy Homes prior to moving to Baltimore, because my aunt Ethel lived there, on the corner of Argyle and Hoffman. Aunt Ethel, who resembles Florida Evans from TV's *Good Times*, had a warm heart and an open door much like my mother. I loved coming down to visit her during the hottest summers. Baltimore had a comfortable, homely feeling that wraps around you, even when surrounded by strangers. People gravitated toward this charm, hence the nickname Charm City.

I leaped out of the U-Haul van to get a better look at the neighborhood. Behind our moving truck was a red minivan with sliding doors. Piled up neatly in both vehicles was the sum of our New York lives. I started helping my mom unpack and noticed this kid standing in the middle of my block. He was just staring at us in confusion, before he slowly started moving in our direction.

"Yo, what's up?" he said. "What kind of part is that in your head?"

I had just gotten a half-moon carved into my fade like the rappers Nas and Raekwon had, with *Red Hook Projects* in the back.

"Don't y'all get parts down here?" I asked.

He shrugged. "I guess. Not like that, though," he answered, taking stock of my haircut, admiring my barber's effort with a look of approval. "That's y'all house?"

"Yeah," I answered. "You live around here?"

"Yeah, man," he said. "I'm Ill. I just moved around here a couple months ago. You need some help with that stuff?"

And just like that, I made my first friend. Ill and I carried all of my things into the house. He even helped me get my dresser up the narrow stairwell and into my bedroom. We ended up hanging out all day, talking about Murphy Homes, the candy store, the Robert C. Marshall Recreation Center, school, and what I needed to know about living in Baltimore. In exchange, I told him about New York, my brother Wolf being the best ballplayer in Red Hook, how my brother Jus got blue diamonds in his teeth, and how cool my big cousin Luck was, who would eventually be moving down to Baltimore to live with us.

"My big cousin Luck knows everything. He can fight, hoop, all of that. I can't wait till he gets here!"

"Why they call him Luck?" Ill asked.

"Cuz you lucky to know him." I laughed.

We had a ball. My mom bought us food, and Ill ended up staying at our new place with us the first night. That's a big reason Baltimore is called Charm City: guys like Ill meet you, pull up on you, and show love, just for the sake of showing love. As a New Yorker, I'd call it Southern hospitality, but of course, Baltimoreans don't consider themselves Southerners.

CHAPTER SEVEN

THE RED HOUSE

We were in the red house made up of painted red bricks that were the color of fruit punch. The brick was so bright it felt like you could see our spot from anywhere.

If you walked through the front door, you'd first hit the vestibule. The first living room was also right there. If you kept walking straight, you'd hit the stairs. We had three bedrooms, and there was also a nice basement that ended up being another bedroom, plus an extra living room on the other side of a full eat-in kitchen that was much bigger than our tiny kitchen in Red Hook. Myrtle Avenue was really a come-up in comparison to our New York apartment. A single day in Baltimore made me realize how much people in New York live on top of each other. My New York home that once felt large now seemed tiny, bunched up. I remembered me, Luck, Jus, and Wolf packed into one bedroom, while other cousins were sleeping in the closet at times, with more people on the couch and even some sleeping in the bathroom. Now we had almost too much space: enough to entertain, to stretch out, and even to expand. The house was not only bigger than our old apartment, but we also had fewer residents. Red Hook had Michelle, Luck, Jus, Deek, Wolf, Mom, and me. This big house had just Mom, Deek, Michelle, and me. The house would still feel big when Luck moved in. Actually, the house would probably feel roomy even if Wolf and Jus decided to make Baltimore home.

Our gang quickly settled in, and I hoped my brothers would be making the trip as well. I thought they'd miss us and would want to leave New York once they got a chance. I really missed both of them, but figured I could learn this new city and maybe even give them the lay of the land when they made it down. I just knew they were coming. I needed them to. I pressed both of them on the phone whenever I could. I even got Jus to give me his word, saying, "I promise we'll be there." So that eased the emotions I was feeling at that moment. I had multiple conversations with each individually about this, and they told me they had things to do in New York—business to take care of—so they weren't ready to move to B-more. My job was to wait patiently. But all wasn't lost, because I had my big sister with me, and everybody knew that Michelle was the real star of the family anyway; she always held me down.

Knowing how I looked up to my brothers, Michelle filled the void of their absence. She told me jokes and old Red Hook stories and just showed me that I wasn't alone and everything was going to be okay. What I loved so much about her was the game she had passed down to me. It was never a "I'm your big sister, so you'd better listen to me" type of situation. No, Michelle gave me real game. She showed me how to move with clear examples of the ways in which a real man should carry himself. "Check this, Carmelo. Yo, look at that man," she told me one day, pointing at a stocky, blockheaded dude screaming hysterically at a woman. "Don't ever do no clown shit like that. That nigga is a fuckin' clown! Send yo dumb ass to the circus!" Michelle would say, or something like that.

We watched that couple start throwing blows at each other. I dug into my bag of penny candy, continuing to watch as the sugar melted in my mouth. Another person jumped in the middle of the confrontation, trying to break up the fight.

"Don't you ever do no sucker shit like that," Michelle said. "Don't you ever hit no girl, ever. Don't you do no shit like that."

That wasn't the first or the last time I had witnessed violence. Red Hook was violent, too; stuff kicked off all the time. But Baltimore had a different type of coldness. Violence, pain, and murder were worked into the language—the graffiti, the name. People nicknamed this place Bodymore, Murdaland. Michelle and I used to sit on the front steps all the time; that was our special hangout spot. We'd compare Baltimore to New York and imagine what Jus would be doing here. Where would Wolf wander off to? Cars would drive up and down the street—some stopping, some speeding by. Young dudes my age would be just in and out of the alley, bossing fiends, hitting sales, trading crack and heroin for cash on both sides of our street.

"Yo, look at these lil' niggas," Michelle would say. "Yo, man, these niggas corny. Don't you ever try to do that. Don't you ever try to fit in and be cool with nobody."

Michelle was smart enough to know that I constantly needed to hear about the power of being an individual. Murphy Homes was a war zone. Its nickname was Murda Homes. So many people got caught up, or hurt real bad, or killed because they were trying to fit in, or for yelling at the wrong person, or just for not understanding where we really were and how dangerous this place could be.

The summer we moved to Murphy Homes, a nine-year-old girl named Ebony Scott was murdered and left in a trash bin. She was from New York like me, the Bronx, to be exact. She traveled down to Baltimore to visit some family and never made it back. Another resident was murdered in one of the high-rises a week before that, but that case lost attention due to Scott's case, her being a child and all. Then her case fell out of the news because ten cops had to be rescued by an armored car after snipers located in different towers boxed them, trying to pick them off one by one. Baltimore's big local paper, the *Sun*, had quoted one disgruntled city housing official who said, "What can we do? When you have police officers pinned down by snipers firing automatic weapons, and it takes a tank to rescue them, what the hell do you do? This is a massive, massive problem that we cannot control."

My sister got a sense of the world we had moved into—the drugs, the violence, and everything—in a way that my mom couldn't fully understand because she was older. My brothers couldn't fully understand it because they didn't live here. I was lucky to have Michelle.

"Be careful out here," she told me. "And Luck will be moving down here soon, so we all gotta look out for each other."

CHAPTER EIGHT

ROBERT C

It was summer, and I needed somewhere to go. The only thing I knew about was the blacktop.

My new neighborhood had a court in an alley that I stumbled across. It was uneven and cracked, with grass shooting out of the cement. I wasn't picky, I just wanted to play. I went around there every day, caught some games, and checked out some of the competition. Some of those B-more kids were good, but I held my own against everyone, even the older kids. They were all, like, "Where you from?" and "Shorty, you got handles!" I made a few more visits, and it never failed: everybody from the alley was telling me that I needed to be playing at Robert C. Marshall Recreation Center, which everybody called Robert C for short.

"Yo, Robert C has in-house, you can join the league," they'd say. "Robert C has a football team! Come up Robert C, yo!"

The kids from the neighborhood recruited me in right away, making this Robert C place sound like heaven on earth, so I had to see it. I followed a couple of kids up Dolphin Street, past more narrow row houses that looked like mine, some occupied, some boarded up with plywood. We passed by groups of dope boys and down another path which led us to two off-brown brick buildings connected by a bridge. I wouldn't want to walk across that thing even if it worked.

"Ay, yo, that's Furman right there," a kid said, pointing to one of the buildings. "That's the school we go to around here, and Robert C is right there on the other side."

We ran over to the entrance and walked inside the gym. It was huge, sticky, and smelled like summer. It was full of kids, packed from one end to the other. Everybody inside was running around and having a good time. This was the energy I needed to be around, the energy that made Baltimore feel like a home. There were six rims that hung above the tattered blond floors, with full-court games happening in every direction.

"Who got next?" I asked.

One of the kids popped up off the floor. He recognized me from the alley, and I was on. There really wasn't any structure or hard rules to the chaotic pickup games, it was just get in where you fit in.

Basketball and most other sports came naturally to me. Even though I was only eight, I was really good and flashy, with a New York game. They say New Yorkers will run around dribbling the air out of the ball with too many crosses, in-and-outs, and hesitations— and there may be some truth in that. But I was embarrassing all of my opponents, sliding them, shaking them, and dropping them with all the moves I picked up in Red Hook. Everybody noticed, and they knew I could get a bucket, because that's what I did over and over again.

"That new boy can score his ass off!"

It didn't take long for word about me to get out. I quickly went from being the kid nobody knew to people mumbling, "That's the kid from that New York family that moved around Myrtle. Shorty gotta game, he really solid, for real."

One of the quick first lessons I learned in Baltimore was that being good in basketball can't save you. Now, I'd been in town for a few weeks, and even though I had been spending every second at Robert C, I didn't really know too many people. I was still trying to figure out my neighborhood. My lesson started with a red shoestring keychain.

I had lost a set of keys, so my mom replaced them. She approached me sitting on the front steps, saying, "You lose these, you ain't getting no more!" She was so loud about it that a group of kids overheard her, and they started laughing.

"I won't lose them," I said. I was still thinking about my dad's necklace, still angry that I basically gave it away. "I promise."

I was determined to hold on to them, so I put the keys on a red string, tied the tightest knot that could be tied, so tight that air couldn't slip through, and wore that shoestring everywhere to do everything, except shower and play basketball. Before getting on the court, I'd take my homemade key necklace off and place it by the wall.

This kid Avon, who happened to be one of the kids who overheard Mom getting on me about the keys in the first place, saw where I put them and swiped them. He just picked them up and exited the Rec. At that point, the only thing I could think of was how my mom was going to kill me. *Where's the keys at?* I'm thinking, *She is literally going to kill me.* She told me not to lose them, and instantly I lost them. I walked back to my block, angry, both of my fists balled up. Everybody knew Avon had the keys. Somehow I went from being the New York kid with unlimited potential to being a joke in a matter of minutes. Then Avon walked around the corner cheesing, spinning my keys around like a propeller, laughing and joking. You would think the key opened up a safe with a million dollars inside, but it just opened our front door. All the other kids—kids I'd never even seen before—started to form a crowd. They had their commentary and *OHHHHs* and *AHHHHs*, and they were just waiting for me to attack Avon. Everybody was waiting, and I understood I had to do it. Was I hard enough to get my keys back or not? This was my neighborhood moment. The new kid, the bully, and a thousand-degree summer day. I'd watched a lot of karate flicks and professional wrestling. *I can beat Avon*, I thought.

"Gimme my keys back!" I said, charging toward Avon, who was moving around and playing with the shoestring. The kids continued laughing, *OHHHH*ing, and *AHHHH*ing.

"I don't got your keys," Avon replied, with my red shoestring visibly swinging from his neck.

"Yo, stop playin', man! Let me get my keys!" I yelled. By now, you could probably see steam shooting from my ears and nostrils.

I lunged at him, reaching for the keys, and he took off the shoestring saying, "Hey, you want it?" He acted like he was throwing it up in the air. When I looked up, he swung on me, and we started to tussle, but he broke away, escaping with my keys.

I went home defeated. Not because of the fight—neither of us won—but because I didn't get my keys back. One thing I want people to understand is that news in neighborhoods like Murphy Homes travels quickly. By the time I got home, my mom was, like, "Boy what's wrong with you? Who are you fighting, and where is your keys?" The ladies at the top of the block were like their own news reporting outlet, telling everybody everything. Remember, this was before cell phones, text messages, social media, and all of that—but gossip and information spread just as quickly.

"Come on, you ain't coming in this house till you fight him every single day," my mother declared. She was still wearing her work clothes, dragging me out the front door. One thing my mother didn't do was allow her kids to be bullied. She didn't play that. She believed in working hard and then working even harder to keep what was yours.

"Ma, I just fought him!" I said.

"If you are not going fight every single day, boy, you going to cry every single day. Now, come on!"

I marched back up the block toward Avon. I knew my mom was watching, and by this time the crowd had tripled. He was still posted, playing with my keys. I lunged at him, grabbed him, flung him to the ground, and whupped on him until some other kids broke up the fight. There's something about your mom watching you fight that gives you an extra jolt of energy. I felt like people who lost fights in front of their moms never got dinner or hugs again. I pulled away from the people holding me back, and I tried to hit him again, but it was over. I had gotten my keys back.

"Okay, little homie," said an older dude wearing a baseball cap. "Little New York ain't afraid to fight, and that's what's up."

I mean-mugged the dude. I didn't know him; maybe he wanted to fight, too. Instead, he extended his hand.

"My name Woody, Shorty. They call me Big Hand Wood," he said. Giving me a pound, he said, "We see you ain't no chump, that's wassup."

The next day, Avon apologized. One of his friends told me about some other things that were going on at the Rec. Before you knew it, I only went to the Rec. It became my second home. Robert C was my outlet. Every single day, I'd wake up, wash my face, brush my teeth, and head to the Rec. Sometimes I even forgot to eat breakfast. That place was full of fun activities. There I signed up for in-house basketball, Pop Warner football, and baseball. The Rec was everything, and most important, it kept me out of trouble. It kept me active, and it got even better when Luck finally showed up in Baltimore.

"Chello, I'm here, baby," Luck said, standing in the doorway of our home. "The spot look good, bro!"

I ran up on him, giving him a big bear hug. I had known he was coming, but I didn't realize it would be so soon. In that moment, I felt like a big part of me that had been missing was suddenly complete. Something about having him in Baltimore made me feel protected and invincible, like nothing bad could happen to me—and suddenly, our new home didn't feel so new anymore. Probably because Luck ushered in the familiarity I needed to adjust fully.

Luck didn't waste any time getting to know Baltimore. He walked everywhere, even all up in neighborhoods that he wasn't supposed to be in. He got into a couple of fights right off the bat, because he didn't understand the dynamic of Baltimore neighborhoods. Baltimore is not a place where you can roam freely. Baltimoreans don't even walk like New Yorkers. New Yorkers will walk forty blocks like it's nothing, whereas the Baltimore blocks are different. They're spaced out in a lot of places, and often they don't even lead to anything. In New York, you'd stumble upon delis, cafés, and all types of interesting places. In Baltimore, it's just more 'hoods and more blocks. But the excessive walking and the fights were good for Luck. With him, it was all about basketball, and those kinds of activities only made him stronger.

At that point, Luck was super nice on the court. He was even better than I remembered him being back in Red Hook. The way he'd stepped up his game made me want to be better. He used to go play games on the court directly in front of the 1058 building in Murphy Homes. I'd see him doing wild crossovers and spin moves that led to rim-shaking dunks. Unlike most people, he played defense. He liked the strapdown, getting all up in your grill and slapping the concrete, reaching for the ball, like, "Come on! Let's go!" The neighborhood guys loved his game. They heard his accent and started calling him New York. I was his little cousin, so I was Lil' New York.

We used to do our thing on the Murphy Homes courts, and then sometimes we'd travel. We'd go to the neighboring and sometimes rival projects called Lexington Terrace, and we'd give those dudes work, too. I'd tail Luck through the split between the 900 building to get over to Lexington Terrace, or what we called the Terrace, where we'd land on the court. There were some cool dudes over there and some assholes, too. But it was all competition, so we pressed them and continued to get better. Eventually, Luck and I joined a league over at the Terrace, both representing the Murphy Homes team. I always played the first game because I was younger. Then I'd watch Luck do his thing once the sun went down and the older kids performed under the bright court lights. Everybody was loving the guy from New York. They were imitating his handles and saying, "That kid Luck from New York, he's gonna make it! He's gonna be in the NBA!" I agreed, and not because Luck was my cousin. He was really that good, ridiculously good, too good for a teenager.

Balling with Murphy Homes had established us as somebodies in that neighborhood. Once we put on Murphy Homes jerseys, we were seen as a part of that group. Being from Murphy Homes and balling with their team came with all kinds of social capital, the kind of social capital you needed to survive in a city like Baltimore. Like I said, sports can't save you. People have no problem shooting an athlete. At the same time, using sports to connect with the neighborhood does help. From that point on, we both started hanging proudly in those projects. We were Murphy Homes, and Murphy Homes was us.

CHAPTER NINE

CARMELO

In the fall, I enrolled in the third grade at Furman L. Templeton, school 125. Templeton was different from the school I attended in New York. New York is synonymous with diversity—a rainbow mix of people representing every different race and ethnic group. I'd see them all when Mom would take us into the city, but Red Hook projects had all Black and Brown people. In Baltimore, everybody was Black except the police; I didn't even see any Puerto Ricans. I thought I might be the only Puerto Rican in Baltimore (or half Rican, anyway). And even though I looked like a regular Black kid, my cover would be blown when they heard my name, Carmelo. *You ever met a Black dude named Carmelo?*

I once looked up my name, and it said, "Carmelo as a boy's name is pronounced kar-MAY-loh. It is of Italian and Hebrew origin, and the meaning of Carmelo is 'orchard; garden.' Biblical place name: refers to Mount Carmel in Israel, which is referred to in ancient writings as a kind of paradise." Despite my name, I didn't feel like I was a part of any paradise. I was a lost kid tossed into a sea of strangers in a new school—so I decided to be a new version of myself. Instead of Carmelo, I called myself Tyrone Johnson. I lied to the school, my teachers, everyone—and told them my name was Tyrone Johnson.

Why Tyrone? Tyrone would be easy, I thought. One thing about the name Carmelo is that everybody messes it up. People would call me everything from Corolla to Car-Mayo—seemed like they'd call me *everything* except Carmelo. Even sometimes back in Red Hook, teachers used to say, "Car what? You got to write your name on an index card." I wouldn't have to do that with the name Tyrone. Everybody knows a Tyrone. And the Tyrone thing even worked for a couple of days, until I got suspended for playing around in class and not doing my homework for multiple days.

This was the '90s, before everybody had the internet, texting, and all of that stuff. Back then, they'd first send you home with a letter. I balled that letter up and slam-dunked it like Clyde Drexler into one of the city trash cans. Next, they'd call your home. I knew the school would always call home around four o'clock. So I'd rush home, knowing that Mom and Deek were going to be at work, and I left the phone off the hook so that callers would get a busy signal and no messages could be left. My mom and stepdad never knew I got suspended.

Even though I was suspended, I got up early the next morning, cleaned myself up, threw my clothes on, grabbed my book bag, and strolled out the front door as if I were headed to school. "See you later," I said to Michelle. I even went onto the schoolyard to mix in with some of the other kids, acting like I was going in. But after the bell rang, I stayed outside for like forty-five minutes, not really knowing what to do. Should I go home? Should I go hoop? I decided on basketball, so I left the schoolyard and headed back home to grab a change of clothes. My school had a little brick wall, near the exit, that I had to peek my head over to make sure the coast was clear. I walked over and placed both of my hands on the wall. I looked left and right, and up the block I saw my mom marching up Pennsylvania Avenue toward Dolphin, with an angry expression on her face.

"Carmelo!" she yelled, picking me up off my feet. "Why aren't you in school?"

I couldn't lie; she was already upset. "I'm sorry, Ma," I said. "I was suspended."

"Suspended!"

She pulled me toward the school, and we both landed in the principal's office. The secretary seated us in a small waiting area. I just looked away and hoped not to cause any more trouble. The principal poked her head out.

"Ms. Johnson, you can come into the office."

"Ms. Johnson?" my mom said, looking at me. "Who's that?"

I shrugged, and we both walked into the office, taking seats in front of the principal.

"I apologize for having you come in, but your son Tyrone has his hands in everything. Now, Tyrone is very intelligent, but—"

"My son Tyrone?" Mom said, confused.

"Yes, Tyrone Johnson," the principal answered, looking at me.

"Tyrone? I don't have a son named Tyrone, and my name isn't Johnson. This boy's name is Carmelo!"

The principal laid me out, Mom joined in, and when we got home, I had to tell her why I had lied. The only good thing that came from this whole situation was that it was the first time I got to tell my mom how I really felt about my name.

"Why is my name Carmelo? I don't like it. Nobody has that name."

"Nobody has it because you are special. If your father knew that you were saying that, if your father was here." She paused. "You wouldn't be saying that. He was an amazing person. You'd better cherish his name."

Honestly, I had never thought about it like that. I had never contemplated what my dad would say about my name, about *our* name. Dad would probably have all kinds of crazy stories about the Carmelo name, anecdotes that he could have passed down to me, and I could have made them my own. But I guess those stories had died with him. He had been gone for so long, and nobody was really talking about him. Sure, his name would come up, but it was all surface things. I wasn't getting the personal, intricate, fun experiences that a dad shares with his son. Maybe if I'd had more stories about the Carmelo name and what it meant to my dad, then I would have been prouder. But my mom's look shook me to my core. It told me that I needed to be prouder. In the moment, she had felt something so strong that she chose the word "cherish." The name Carmelo meant something. Mom's words and actions had shown me that. Even though I didn't fully understand, I vowed never again to disrespect my given name.

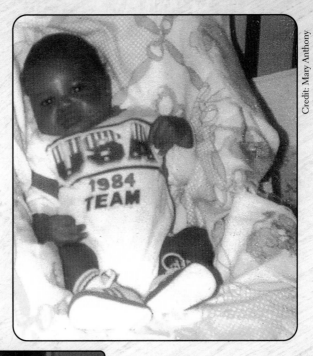

One-month-old
baby Melo.

A dapper one-year-old.

A happy kid at one and
a half years old.

All dressed up for a
family photo at
two years old.

Family photo with
my mother, Mary;
sister, Michelle;
and brother, Jus.
Where's Wolf?

PAL Miccio Head Start class picture, 1989.

Red Hook Community Center,
PAL Miccio Head Start
graduation, 1989.

With my
godfather,
Bum Bum,
at Head Start
graduation, 1989.

Holding up my Head
Start diploma and award
certificate, 1989.

Pre-K picture day, 1989.

PS 27 Pre-K class picture, 1989.

Accepting an award at
Mount Royal awards banquet.

Celebrating with my
nephew Wayne and his
dad after Mount Royal's
awards ceremony.

With my mother, Mary, and sister, Michelle, at Mount Royal's awards banquet.

AAU Nationals at Disney's Wide World of Sports at Madison Rec Center.

Am I my brother's keeper? With brothers Jus and Wolf, and cousin Tavares, on the night that Luck was killed.

Found my mother in the stands after winning the NCAA National
Championship in New Orleans for Syracuse University, 2003.

CHAPTER TEN

FILLING VOIDS

Every night ended the same way every morning began, with me thinking about my brothers moving down to Baltimore so we could be a family again. Jus was locked up, so that wasn't happening for him, but we used to have calls all the time. I'd tell him about Robert C and all the dudes I had been meeting down in Baltimore. I shared how I was doing my thing in baseball, basketball, and football. He would always tell me to be aware of surroundings, pay attention to how people move, and realize that everything that looks the same ain't the same. It's crazy how much more I communicated with Jus, who was behind the wall, than with Wolf, who was free. But finding Wolf was like finding Waldo, you know? He always has been a catch-me-if-you-can kind of guy. Wolf didn't have a phone, a pager, none of that. To find him, you really had to go to New York. But at least Luck was here now, so things were looking up.

Luck enrolled in St. Frances Academy over in East Baltimore. The reason was the coach there was a close family friend named Eric Skeeters, or "Skeets." He always promised to look out for Luck and me, and for the most part he did. Luck was focused and seemed ready to take basketball seriously—really, really seriously. I came onto the St. Frances team as a ball boy, so I had front-row seats to the Luck show every week. Seeing him in that jersey made me proud.

At that time, there was a famous flashy New York guard, from Queens to be exact, who handled the rock like a yo-yo. He was slashing in between defenders, getting to the rack whenever he wanted, and always finding the open man with ease. Honestly, it seemed that dude was so cool he never even broke a sweat. His name was Kenny Anderson. Anderson was a big deal everywhere, but especially to New York kids like us. College recruiters were on him since he was in middle school. He even caught the front page of the New York City sports section at fourteen. Anderson went on to win every award that a high school basketball player could get, including being named New York State Mr. Basketball, McDonald's All-American, and Player of the Year by Gatorade, just to mention a few. How did I know all of this? Because Luck knew all of this. Kenny Anderson was his favorite player, so he was one of my favorite players, too.

Luck idolized Anderson and played just like him. Posters of Anderson wearing number 12 at Georgia Tech lined our basement walls. Luck had cut out magazine articles about when Kenny was drafted to the Nets. Kenny was his guy. And people from the neighborhood knew, too. If they weren't calling Luck New York, then they were definitely calling him Kenny Anderson, and my big cousin didn't disappoint. It didn't matter if he balled in his school uniform or was wearing Timbs, he could cross you, leave you, whip back, and drop you. That's why I always laughed at dudes who needed a certain type of shoe, an NBA headband, and matching cushioned socks to play, because Luck would crush you in a pair of Buttas, Polo boots, or Mountain Gears. In the Bronx, they even called him Boots, because he used to play in jeans and Timbs all the time, destroying everyone in his path.

Luck owned Last Court. Last Court was so named because it was the last court on the outskirts of the projects. Walk across Last Court, and then you would pass Howard Street and the state building and be headed toward downtown. I used to love running up there, because all the kids in the neighborhood would say, "Lil' New York, your cousin on the court getting busy!" We'd watch Luck work—he'd be there shirtless, wearing jeans, jumping like he had springs in his boots, knocking down forty-footers, and it always looked easy. I didn't see Luck every day. He lived with us, but he was a grown man trapped inside a teenager's body. Like all men, he needed to explore, conquer, and leave his mark on other places. He'd leave the house and venture off to discover Baltimore and figure out the city for himself. I imagine he was out making and meeting girls, seeing how Baltimoreans lived, and imagining his life as an adult. He was determining what this city, or any city, had to offer a Black man like himself. I just knew that when he came around, I had to be ready.

"Yo, Chello, come on. We going to the court," Luck would say, busting into my bedroom and waking me up. "Yo, we going to the court. Come on, we out." I'd pop up, wiping the dried sleep out of my eyes and reaching for my sneakers, knowing that he and I were about to battle down 77. That court, 77, was where we used to work out, the court where the bulk of my scars came from.

If I was taking too long, Luck would reiterate, "Yo, we going to the court. Come on, let's go get some shots in. Come on, Chello!"

Those battles down 77 were some of the worst in my life. He used to foul me, push me, and slam my head down into the pavement. The double rims 77 had made it tough to hit jumpers during the day and even harder at night. Not that it mattered, because Luck would block all of my shots anyway. "Gimme that shit!" he'd say as he shouldered me, elbowed me, crushed me. I'd be wanting to cry, and he'd clip me, like, "Yo, you better not cry!"

Crying was not allowed. As a matter of fact, crying was the worst thing you could do. We were men, and men don't cry. That's when I really started learning that I had to do whatever it took to win. He slapped me, and I slapped him back. I ate his elbows and popped right back up after his pushes, letting the blood from my scrapes dry and scab over, spitting the dirt out of my mouth, ignoring the pain, fighting harder and harder. I was too little to win, but at least I wasn't going out like a *sucka*. Luck was the best basketball player in the neighborhood, and everybody knew it. He was going to make it, and if I wanted his respect, I had to fight as though I was going to make it, too. We had these battles over and over again, and I got better.

My mom didn't mind if Luck grabbed me late at night or at the crack of dawn. She saw that we were starting to know everybody in the neighborhood. She was happy that I was into sports at a time when many of the kids in our neighborhood were getting lost in those streets. Meantime, I was at the Rec or playing baseball or hooping with Luck. My stepdad, on the other hand, didn't really take interest in my athletics, because he was too busy being upset at everything. This was one angry brother. Anything could make him mad, even sunshine and flowers. Who gets mad at sunshine and flowers?

Wilfred Huggins was his name, but we called him Deek. Deek was around before my dad and is actually Wolf's, Michelle's, and Jus's biological pops. I imagine Deek and my mom had got into it, for whatever reason. They decided to split, or she left him—leaving space for my dad to come into the picture and make me—only for her to end up reconnecting with Deek after my dad's untimely demise. With my real dad dying so early, I can honestly say that Deek was always there as far as I can remember. I grew up with him in the household from Red Hook to Baltimore. He was there, but just unnecessarily angry all the time. Even Richard Pryor couldn't make that dude laugh. I literally had never seen him smile before.

"Goddamn it, cut the shit!" he'd say if I ever bounced the ball in the house. I knew you shouldn't bounce a ball indoors, but if I dropped my ball by mistake, he'd still lose it. "Come on, man, what the hell is this? What we doing? Goddamn!"

Deek made me hate being in that house. It was like living with James Evans from *Good Times*, the disgruntled and frequently unemployed father character, except this was real life, and there were no snappy jokes to deflect the poverty and pain. A day in the house with Deek meant you were sentenced to deprivation. He was angry and cheap and prided himself on being a hard-nosed Black man.

"Why all these lights on?" he'd yell if there was ever more than one switched on.

"Hey, Carmelo, turn that goddamn music off," he'd say, even if it wasn't loud.

"All right, all right, cool," I'd always answer.

My mother was working two jobs at the time, so when Luck wasn't around, I was stuck in the house with Deek. I was always in a hurry to get out of there, even if the Rec was closed, even if it was ten degrees outside. I had to get away from that man. Getting away was easy because I had the Rec, and I also tied myself up with enough sports to avoid him almost completely. I also made friends in the neighborhood, mainly two guys who loved sports as much as I did: Lil' Kenny and Big Duke.

CHAPTER ELEVEN

KENNY AND DUKE

Big Duke lived on my block, he went to elementary school 125 with me, and we played baseball together. He was the back catcher when I played pitcher and first baseman, so that's how we connected. True to his name, Duke was big in stature, with an even bigger smile. He was larger than life, always cool, full of vitality and jokes, and down for whatever. I'd make fun of Duke, and he'd make fun of me, until we laughed so hard that we cried real tears and we couldn't even breathe. For us to act serious, you'd have to pay us, and we'd still probably laugh our way out of the deal. Duke and I walked to 125 every day. He'd jump up bright and early, knock on my door, and then we'd be out. On our way to school, we were always talking about sports, the teams we played for, the teams we wanted to play for, and how we were going to get there.

Kenny went to a different school, 122, but he was still in the picture. We connected more as my interest in basketball increased. He was a short, natural point guard who could outscore anybody. What Kenny lacked in height he made up in heart, and what he lacked in heart he made up in candy. Kenny and I ate enough candy to rot every tooth in the whole of West Baltimore. We tore the candy store down all the time. Eating candy was actually all we wanted to do some days. After practice, before practice, or in the middle of practice, it didn't matter—we needed penny candy, Twizzlers, Now and Laters, Jolly Ranchers, and Lemonheads. We would take bags of it over to his place. I stayed there a lot and told him everything about missing my brothers, about my angry stepdad, about everything. Kenny had a way of understanding things about me that most of the people in my life didn't really get. He was the first peer I told about my real dad. He understood, because he lost his mom around the same age. Kenny's dad was not around, and he lived with his grand-mother. Even though he didn't really show it, he experienced as much pain as I did. Our pain was our connection.

The three of us linked up and became inseparable. If Duke or Kenny needed me, or if I needed them, regardless of the situation, we would be there, ready to hold each other down. I remember there was one time during the blizzard of '96 when we were out in the street play-ing football. "Yo, look at that!" I said. I pointed at a group of dope boys on the other end of the block stomping out a junkie. Somehow the fiend was able to break free and blasted up the block toward us.

"Yo, stop him! Grab him!" one of the dope boys yelled at me and Duke.

Now, this dude was flying! It looked like somebody had shot him out of a cannon, and Duke and I stood there with our mouths hanging wide open.

Duke and I were just little kids, so there was nothing we could really do about it. This guy was a grown man. But still, Duke jumped in front of him, and the guy spun, blasted up the street, and collapsed. The dope boy who was chasing him had finally caught up. He walked toward us with a big stick in his hand, like, "Why didn't y'all grab him?"

Before we could answer, the dude started hitting me and Duke with the stick.

We took off!

"Get the fuck over here!" he yelled.

I ran one way, and Duke went the opposite. When the dude got close to Duke, I ran toward him so that he would chase me instead, and Duke did the same.

"Why y'all ain't grab him? Why ain't y'all grab him?" the guy continued, swinging his stick at us.

Eventually, our older friend L noticed the situation and said, "Nah, yo. That's my man. That's Duke and Melo. Chill, chill!"

The guy looked at us in disgust. Duke and I laughed as we headed back down the street. Duke's uncle eventually went down to the bottom of the block and squashed the whole thing. He explained that we were good kids and didn't need to be caught up in all that. You had to pass a gauntlet—of gangsters, dice games, stickup kids, rats, and fiends—to even get to me and Duke. There were plenty of people in the neighborhood looking for trouble, so trying to recruit us would always turn out to be a waste of time. Too many things like that were happening on our block anyway, so we moved our whole operation into the alley.

Duke, Kenny, and I built a makeshift basketball goal out of a crate and plywood in the alley. Our neighborhood was full of real basketball courts, but the alley felt like our own world, a small private club which only we were invited to. We started spending more time back there, as opposed to on the block. In the alley, we had our small backyard and a little patchy field that we played football on. In the summer, we even had a little pool to climb into on hot days. There was still some action at the top of the alley—dope boys hitting sales out of the hole, crack on one side, heroin on the other, giving out testers, and people who couldn't hustle in the projects working the block. But it was still more peaceful in the alley. The front had completely lost control. There was prostitutes running up and down the block, asshole cops who picked on us for nothing, crews beefing over territory, and constant confusion. The alley was an oasis on the concrete. It allowed us to avoid all of that negativity. It was one of the few places where we could keep our sanity.

"Chello, let me holla at you!" Luck said one day. I was headed out the front door, on my way to meet Kenny at the Rec. "We need to rap, B."

"You wanna get some shots up?" I asked. "I'm headed to Rec now, but we can slide wherever."

Luck looked down at his scuffed boots, surveyed the room, looked back up, and then said, "Yo. I'm not feeling that dumbass Catholic-school shit. Skeets's on some dumb shit, so I quit."

"What?" I asked, confused. "Yo, what happened?"

"Don't make a big deal about it, Chello. I'm gonna go home for a while to see some people, get some things in order. Then I'll come right back down here and get to it, probably with another school. I'm telling you this because I wanna make sure you good. You good?"

"I mean . . . ?"

"I'm coming right back. Keep working on ya game, don't let up."

All I could do was sit there, hold my ball, and say, "Okay." I mean, this was Luck—my guy, the best basketball player in the neighborhood, the best ballplayer I knew, my big cuz, the guy responsible for grooming me. I wished him well and prepared to survive while anticipating his triumphant return.

You know how they say "When it rains, it pours?" I felt like that was happening to me, because then I found out that I was losing Michelle as well. She was pregnant, needed her own space, and found a house a couple of miles away. One by one, my family was all spreading out, without me. But even though I was crushed that Luck was leaving and that Michelle was moving out, I was happy to be getting a new family member. Plus Michelle's old bedroom, so I guessed all wasn't lost. I also knew Luck was coming back. By the time he returned to Baltimore, I'd be more solid, more respected, more complete.

CHAPTER TWELVE

THE BALLPLAYER

The first organized basketball team I played for was Robert C. We weren't a traveling team, we were local. We went to war in the Rec during multiple in-house leagues or against other recs that we could walk to. By the time our season started, everybody already knew I was good, someone to pay attention to. Watching Wolf as a little kid made me as tough as nails; getting cracked and knocked on the ground by Luck made me even tougher. We shot jumpers on double rims at night, so imagine how easy it was to score on a regular rim in an indoor gym against kids in my age group. Even though I was so young, I was already a force to be reckoned with.

While doing my thing at Robert C, I joined the Madison Buccaneers. Skeets, the coach at St. Frances Academy, lived across the street from Madison Rec over on Biddle Street. He was also the JV coach and was the person who got Luck into the school before he quit and went back to New York. Skeets helped him enroll and get set up with his classes and everything. I thought maybe he could do it again if Luck had a change of heart and came back. He believed in Luck before anybody else did. Sometimes I used to go to his house with Luck. I'd play outside, meet dudes from East Baltimore, work on my crossover and my jump shot, and practice everything else that Luck taught me.

A West Baltimore kid venturing to East Baltimore was unheard of, but I was from New York, so I didn't know any better. People always think that there is this big beef between East and West Baltimore, but that's not it. The problem is transportation. Public transportation in Baltimore is so bad that a five-minute car ride from East Baltimore to West Baltimore will take three hours by bus. That means those two sides never really communicate. At the time, I think the Baltimore subway only had four or five stops. Compare this to New York, which has the best public transportation system in the world, with countless stops that touch every borough, neighborhood, and block. East and West Baltimore are basically the same—they deal with the same poverty, the same poor schools, the same housing issues, the same racist cops from the same police force, and they are both full of Black people trying to make it. Any dudes with a car from West Baltimore loved people from East Baltimore, and vice versa. Because I was the water boy and ball boy at St. Frances, everybody from both sides of Baltimore got to know me. A legendary coach named Sarge, who ran the Madison Buccaneers program, noticed me out playing one day. He caught wind of my talent, and just like that, I was on my first traveling team. Sarge even had a spot for me to play in the regionals, and if we won, I'd get to fly to Florida. We won, and just like that, I was going. It almost didn't seem real: one day I'm hanging in the alley, playing 21 or 50 putout at the Rec, and the next day I'm boarding an airplane to play against kids from other cities just like NBA players do? I'd never dreamed of getting on an airplane, and then boom! Basketball put me on an airplane—instantly and for free.

Baltimore/Washington International Airport was huge. It was full of hallways that went in every direction and never seemed to stop, and the bathrooms were like a mile apart. I wasn't the only one on that trip who had never been on an airplane before. Some of my teammates were scared to fly, but I was just ready to go. It was a perfect way to kill time while Luck was gone, and it got me away from my stepdad. I often wondered if his anger subsided when I wasn't around. Did he only became enraged when he looked at me, seeing the face of another man? Constantly being reminded that my mom had a child with a person who was not him? I imagined that if I was Deek's blood, he would have brought me to the airport and celebrated my new basketball success. I imagined he would have been nice and supportive and loved me the same way he loved my older siblings. But that wasn't up to me, that was up to him. And dwelling on the way he treated me wasn't going to help anybody. Either way, I decided early on that his anger wasn't going to kill any basketball opportunities for me. I wasn't going to let it dampen my first experience with luxury. I stopped by a mirror to check out my new uniform, new sneakers, new backpack—all clean, pristine, and courtesy of the Rec, because I could play basketball. I was about to get on an airplane, and Deek would probably never be able to fly. That fact probably added to his anger. I was from a neighborhood where nobody got on airplanes. We were from the bottom. Nobody was ashamed of it, because everybody knew that everybody was broke. Hearing about kids who ate their cereal with a fork to save milk was normal. Waking up with a sore throat because you used the oven to heat up your place was normal. Fifteen people in a one-bedroom was normal. Airplanes? Not normal. Moments like these really mattered to kids like me. I was going to enjoy every second of it.

Being in the airport felt so good. Getting on the plane, walking past all the shops, the pilots, and the flight attendants. Being with all my teammates, my crew, even though I didn't know a lot of the East Baltimore kids. Our matching book bags, Madison-branded tracksuits, and Nikes unified us. We were one.

"Where you all from?" people kept asking.

"Baltimore!" we responded proudly.

"West, though." I laughed, joking with my eastside teammates. "I'm from Baltimore West, to be exact!"

Even though I played with Madison for that one tournament, I was still Robert C to the bone. That was home.

The one other time I ventured away from Robert C was to play in a Baltimore–DC game. It was put together by a slick older dude named Robert "Bay" Frazier from East Baltimore. Bay whipped a BMW with blue lights, which was something I had never seen before. He used to set up basketball games all over Baltimore and DC as well. Bay was a true fan of the game, hungry to share his basketball knowledge with everybody, and he always brought a younger crew to play in a little preliminary game before the big boys hit the court. Mike Lloyd was a superstar guard from Dunbar High who made it all the way up to Syracuse. He was supposed to be playing, and Bay allowed me to roll all the way to DC with him. When our junior game was over, I would go to the concession stand for Bay and the rest of the older guys. I'd get snacks, chips, soda, iced teas, whatever they wanted, and they'd let me keep the change. "Lil' Melo, come here," Bay would say. "You gotta couple dollars in ya pocket, don't blow, stack it." And I listened. It was a good hustle and a way for me to meet the best older players from Baltimore. I wasn't trying to be like them, but I was intrigued with that world. I saw the special treatment they received for being good at sports, the way girls swooned over them. They weren't in the NBA, but they were still kings. I had a whole lot of respect for them.

In between sports and just playing around, Duke, Kenny, and I decided that we needed to make some money. My mom provided me with everything I needed—a roof, hot meals, and school uniforms—but I wanted some things, too. You know, all the extras. We used to sit out on the stoop and watch the dope boys roll up and down the pavement with new Barkleys (CB34 was my favorite), the new Pippens or More Uptempos, Air Force 1s, New Balance 990s or 991s or 1300s, and whatever type of Jordans. I wanted all of that plus new Polo shirts, Polo jackets, hoodies, bubble coats, Nautica, Hilfiger.

I didn't have a lot, but I really knew what I liked. I could probably trace it back to that one Easter when my mom had bought me some white and maroon KJs. They were the signature Converse shoe for high-flying Phoenix Sun point guard Kevin Johnson. Everybody had the black ones or the white and purple ones that matched KJ's uniform, but I had maroon and white. KJ himself probably didn't even have maroon and white. I swear, I put those on and shut down the whole fucking world. They were leather with a strap and REACT Juice. The REACT Juice, which was a greenish gel-like substance located on the heel of each shoe, was part of the marketing; it was supposed to be responsible for making Johnson so explosive. The image of his 6'1" frame face-to-face dunking on a 7' Hakeem Olajuwon lived in my head, rent-free, forever. Did I think the REACT Juice would make me fly like that? Absolutely not, but it couldn't hurt. To sweeten the deal, my mom grabbed me a white Polo shirt with a maroon horse that matched the shoes perfectly. In that moment, I realized looking good made you feel good, regardless of what was happening around you. I was surrounded by an open-air drug market where murder happened weekly, but still, looking good equaled feeling good. So if you ever hear a person passing judgment on a dude from the projects dressed in expensive clothes from head to toe, know that maybe it's the only way he knows how to make himself feel good. In a neighborhood devoid of therapy, positive reinforcement, or opportunity, those new Nikes may have made his cold night a little warmer. I always, always wanted clothes to make me feel good about myself. I threw those KJs on, with that new 'Lo and some new khakis, and went down to the Inner Harbor. It was a tourist spot with restaurants and shops overlooking the water in downtown Baltimore. I felt invincible, like the most successful person in the entire world. In order to maintain that feeling, I was willing to do anything.

"Yo, all the money is down on Martin Luther King and Mulberry," Kenny said one day. "All we need is some squeegees and a bucket of water."

"Bucket of water?" I asked.

"Oh, yeah!" Duke chimed in. "They be making a lot of money down there cleaning windows! As long as you don't get slapped by a car!"

"Nah, we'll be careful." Kenny laughed.

That's all I needed to hear. I grabbed a bucket, got a couple of dollars from my mom to buy a squeegee from the gas station, then blasted down to MLK to set up shop. Cars whipped up and down that busy street all day. I imagine the drivers hated catching red lights, but it meant Duke, Kenny, and I and a bunch of other money-hungry project kids were running up on your window. Squeegees in hand, slanging soap everywhere, and then demanding you to pay us for our services which you never even asked for.

And sometimes sweet old ladies would give us a dollar. Angry old white men would fuss at us, like, "Get that shit off of my car!" as we shot middle fingers at their rearviews. Hustlers sometimes would give us a twenty or a fifty and say, "Don't put nothing on my windows, lil' man, but keep working, and one day you gonna get paid." Most days, we went back to the block with just a pocketful of change, but that was enough to energize us to do it again the next day. I had a loose floor plank in my room. I could lift it up and store all of my squeegee proceeds there, along with the allowance I would get sometimes. It was a pretty good hiding place. I never stacked up a fortune, but I definitely had something to hold on to.

After doing this a few times, we started learning what people wanted. You could tell who wanted their windows washed without them saying anything—by their vibe, their energy, and the looks they gave. Some people wanted to help us out, and others seemed like they wanted to run us over, but that was just another day in West Baltimore.

The rules to squeegeeing are pretty simple:

1. Always have a partner, in case something bad happens.
2. Always split the money evenly to be fair and to avoid pointless beef.
3. Change can go in your pocket, but always tuck bills into your sock, in case somebody tries to rob you.
4. Most important, always stay on your side of Mulberry Street. The other side is for the Lexington Terrace dudes. Don't try to fight them over some chump change.

On bad days we'd make about five dollars apiece, and on good ones we pulled in over a hundred. Our little hustle was going well until one of the neighbors caught my mom walking up the block after a long day of work.

"Hey, Mary," she said. "Your son down there on Martin Luther King in the street. I seen Melo down there squeegeeing. Y'all all right over there? Everything good?"

"What? Squeegeeing? What?" my mom answered. "Yeah, all right, we doin' just fine. That wasn't him!"

"I see that boy every day! That's him! I know what Melo look like!"

After that, my mom shut down the squeegeeing. I wasn't too upset about it, because too many little beefs were kicking off with Lexington Terrace. The cops were making us leave the block all the time, and the whole operation just got frustrating. We also got turned on to a new hustle, selling candy out in front of Orioles and Ravens games.

Kenny was the one who came up with the new hustle. We noticed he kept busting out with brand-new Polo shirts, Polo hats, Polo jackets and hoodies, walking around like he knew Ralph Lauren.

"Where you be gettin' all of this money from?" I asked Kenny, admiring his new shirt and Nikes. "You fresh every day, boy!"

"Selling candy," Kenny answered with a calm shrug.

"What? Y'all are just selling candy?" Duke asked. "Really coming back with big packs of money like that?"

We could never make that kind of money squeegeeing, so I was sold, and Duke was, too.

"How can we get on?"

"Check this out," Kenny explained. "This old junkie nigga named Reds, I don't really know him, I honestly don't know who he is or where he come from, but every weekend, he come grab niggas and take us down to the stadium, so just be ready."

The next weekend, an old, beat-up, tired-looking light-skin dude named Reds pulled up in a van and told us to jump in. Against every warning about strangers, candy, and vans, we hopped in the back, laughing, like, "Yo, who is this guy, where he come from, where he get this candy from, and where is he taking us?" Kenny was chill because he already knew that we were about to make a lot of money. The hustle was simple: sell the candy bar for two dollars, take a dollar for ourselves, and give the other dollar to Reds, who had all the candy. He was kind of like a chocolate Escobar, and we were his child soldiers. Worked like a charm.

Reds was loaded with unlimited amounts of candy. I had never seen so much candy in one place at one time. Just looking at it gave me a toothache. All kinds of flavors were on deck—M&M's, Twix, Snickers, Milky Way, 3 Musketeers, Rolos, Milk Duds, Almond Joy, and everything else you can think of. It never ran out, and I wondered where he got it all from. But we didn't ask any questions, we just did our jobs.

I encountered so many fans that first day, and it felt like I wasn't even working that long. I had made a quick sixty dollars, and I couldn't wait to do it again. Dude came back every weekend like clockwork. Every Saturday and every Sunday when there was a home game, he was coming to pick us up. Now, he may have been a drunk with empty liquor bottles covering the entire floor of his ride, smelling like yesterday's yak, with boxes of candy everywhere, but man, that guy was consistent. He was never late, always fully stocked, and completely focused on getting money.

When we had really good days, old Reds would take us to Marshalls. He already knew that we wanted to go buy new Polo shirts. That's all we talked about, all we wanted to wear, and they sold them for as low as fifteen dollars. Some of those Marshalls Polos were a little defective, like the Polo player stitched on the left breast would look a little drunk up there on his horse. We didn't care, we just wanted to be in Ralph Lauren so bad. Lauren also had a cheaper brand called Chaps, but that was flagrant—we wouldn't be caught dead in that. We joked that the brand was an acronym for Couldn't Have a Polo Shirt. From there, we would hit up the mall just in case we had enough left over to get sneakers, too. I needed this. Sometimes I wondered why Reds didn't just sell the candy himself and keep all the money, but then I realized that people like to buy things from kids. When you support a Black kid from the city, it kind of makes you feel like you are making a difference. Customers probably fantasized that we would take the money we made and apply it toward our little United Negro College Funds, but we just wanted clothes. Reds knew what we wanted, and he knew how those people would react toward us, and he capitalized on both.

Before I was making money off these hustles, I sometimes went downtown to different shops to steal new clothes. I'm not proud of this, but I had some dark moments. Duke didn't need to come, because he was kind of spoiled. Both of his parents were taking care of him, and he was also too lazy to walk all the way down to the Gallery to try to get a shirt. Kenny had older brothers and his grandma looking out for him. Having older brothers around meant two things: first, they knew the pressure to be fresh and that looking like a bum was a no-no; and second, even if everybody was broke, you could still borrow their clothes and make an honest attempt at having a rotation. So a lot of times, I was the only one who desperately needed it. I hated stressing my mom out, and I knew Deek wasn't giving me anything but a hard time.

Our hustle with Reds went on for the whole football and baseball season. We stacked up so much money and bought so many new shirts, hats, and pairs of sneakers, and we had a lot of fun at times. Many weekends, Kenny and I had to look out for Duke. He struggled with selling candy—seemed like the fans at the games didn't want to buy from him because they thought he looked like an older Black dude hustling, not realizing that he was a kid like us. Squeegeeing, selling candy, and all of those kinds of hustles only really work when you still look like a child. Once you are no longer adorable, people become a lot less generous.

We never saw Reds after the season ended, and honestly I wasn't really looking for him. Basketball had begun to consume all of my free time. I later heard Reds stopped with the candy hustle because some kids weren't paying him his cut or they found their own candy supply and just moved on without him. That's how hustles work: cop and blow, come and go.

CHAPTER THIRTEEN

BACK AT IT

As the sun dipped into the clouds and night started to creep, I was sitting on the steps with Big Duke. We were talking about my crazy basketball and football schedule, when Big Duke interrupted me to go in the house and grab something to drink. As he walked inside, I saw a dude bopping up the street. He was swinging his arms, wave-like, in both directions, with a duffel bag in one hand, wearing a big smile.

"Yo! Yo!" the voice said.

I squinted my eyes, but the figure was still blurry.

Duke came back outside, asking, "Yo, who is that waving?"

"I don't know," I answered.

"Yo, Chello! Chello!"

When I heard his voice, I said, "Yoooo! That's Luck!" I ran down the street and gave him a big hug. He reeked of stale beer and cigarettes, like he'd been on some type of bender. I immediately began telling him about all the things I'd been doing on the court, how my game had gotten better, how I really *really* had handles, and how I had a couple dollars in my pocket from the candy hustle. I took a step back and looked at him. His eyes were yellowish, and he didn't seem as cut as the Luck I remembered. He seemed beat, out of it, and as if he had left a piece of himself in New York. Something just seemed off.

"I'm happy to see you, too, B." Luck laughed. "New York is wild crazy right now. We gonna hit the court. I'm gonna see this game you talkin' 'bout."

"Let's go!" I said excitedly.

My mom had been hearing things about what Luck was up to in New York, as well as his Baltimore antics, so she was constantly getting on him about being in the streets. "Take care of yourself, Lucky," she'd always say.

He had dropped out of St. Frances or got kicked out or whatever, but now he was back, and we could get a fresh start. Apparently, Luck had gotten into some static in New York, which was easy for me to believe; he was my cousin and role model, but dude was also a hothead. He'd fight anybody. You could even be seven feet tall and three hundred pounds of pure muscle, but if you disrespected Luck or pissed him off, he was going to swing on you. And if his right hook didn't work, then he would come back with a baseball bat. He would keep coming back over and over again until you saw things his way. Luck's mentality was a gift and a curse, because you needed to be tough and stand up for yourself in the 'hood. On the other hand, if you fussed with somebody who was connected to a dangerous block or a gang, you could be killed. This was true in Red Hook and definitely true in Baltimore. In Red Hook, they'd quickly kill you over disrespect, but in Baltimore, they'd kill you for sport.

I was a little older now. I knew the block, the people, the pods that made up my world. Murphy Homes was the center of it all—the kingdom that I could see from my steps. It was full of the people who flooded into my block when I wasn't spilling into theirs, making us one. Big Hand Wood was one of the rulers of this world, and he had respect for me. I hoped that respect would rub off on Luck.

When I first moved to Baltimore, Big Hand Wood was the man running the block. He went to jail, then came home and picked right up where he'd left off. Wood was older and always wore a big smile. It was the same smile he greeted me with when I first moved to Myrtle Avenue and had to fight Avon for stealing my keychain. They called him Big Hand because he could throw hands—Wood could really fight. As I grew older, I learned that you couldn't mention Murphy Homes without mentioning Big Hand Wood. There was a group of dudes running things, but he was the leader of the original Murphy Homes guys. Wood was who everybody looked up to. People moved like him, talked like him, and even joked like him. He caught me in the alley one day hooping on the crate, watching me as I hit bucket after bucket, and was, like, "Shorty, you got heart!"

"Thanks," I said, continuing to shoot.

"Keep ballin', shorty, you gonna be nice enough to hoop wit' us soon."

From that day on, Wood made sure everybody showed me love and looked out for me. At that point, I knew I was good. And now that Luck was back, being my cousin and all, I was sure Wood and all those older dudes would look out for him, too.

Now the city was in the process of tearing down Murphy Homes. The violence had gotten out of control, police officers had lost hope, and many residents just wanted something different. They had already bulldozed the notorious Lafayette housing projects in East Baltimore, and everybody knew that Murphy Homes was next on the list. The city started evacuating everybody from the buildings in preparation for a massive demolition. Older residents were given vouchers to move to Baltimore County or neighborhoods on the suburban outskirts. As the migration from the high-rises began, many of the young dudes, especially Wood and his crew, couldn't see living anywhere else. Not to mention their business was tied to that community; they had set up shop on my block, which was how we met in the alley that day and began our friendship. From that moment on the block of Myrtle Avenue, I would forever be affiliated as a part of Murphy Homes. When I needed something, those Murphy Homes dudes were always there. Wood would even give us a couple of dollars here and there, because he knew we played sports and didn't hustle. They became my family, especially Wood. If somebody was fucking with me, they would handle it instantly. I didn't even have to ask.

We used to go to Shake and Bake on Saturday nights. We called it the

Bake. It was a big roller-skating rink in our neighborhood. It was one of the only things that we young kids could do for fun on a weekend outside of sports and hanging on the block. The Bake was located on Pennsylvania Avenue, right across the street from the dome. Behind it, you had L&D, which was Lawrence and Division, and Sandtown Winchester on the other side. With the skating rink there in the middle, all of these neighborhoods mixed. We loved to go up there—Duke, Kenny, and I would spend whole weeks planning to hit the Bake. And when we did, it was normally peaceful, but sometimes the mix of all those kids from all those different blocks created trouble.

We were there on one of those crazier nights, and I'm not really sure what happened. It could have been over a girl, it could have been some dudes from another neighborhood talking about fighting us. I didn't really ask any questions; I was ready to fight. Duke, Kenny, and I were brothers. If you hit one of us, that meant you had to deal with all of us. So I walked out of the Bake with both of my fists tight, ready to swing on whoever. Right there was Wood.

"Yo, Shorty, get in the car, man." I didn't know what was going on, but I did know he was there to protect us. "Yo, get in the car!" Wood repeated angrily. "Fuck is y'all doing up here?"

Initially, I didn't know why he was so upset, but I later found out that two neighborhoods who had static were supposed to meet at the Bake to settle their problems. Somebody could have gotten stabbed, shot, or even murdered. Wood knew about it, but we didn't know, because we were just kids trying to have fun. Wood was always there, making sure that we got to be kids who didn't have to worry about stuff like that.

This was the kind of community I was happy to be a part of. I wanted to share what I found with Luck, too. He wouldn't have to worry about all the drama in New York, because this Baltimore life was gonna be very, very good to us.

Murphy Homes had me. They also worked extra hard keeping me off the corner. There was no way I was getting close to any drugs, guns, or any of that—not on Wood's watch. He'd see me sniffing around and be, like, "You ain't doing that, go in the house! You got practice tomorrow! You got school tomorrow!"

Wood and the others would hear my mother come to the window and call me in, "Melo, Melo, Melo!"

"Yo, your mom is calling you, man," Wood would say. "Go get your ass in the house!"

That was our relationship. On regular days, I could post up on the block with them, sitting outside hearing stories about Baltimore dudes from back in the day. Dudes who were getting money like Little Melvin or wild shooters like Anthony Jones who would never see the light of day again. They weren't telling me these stories to make me want to be a street guy. They just wanted me to know my city's history and learn from people who made mistakes that they could never make right.

"Yo, run to the store for me real quick," Wood would say.

"All right, cool. What you want?" I'd answer. And I'd go, and he'd allow me to buy something for myself, keep the change, and continue to hang as long as I was doing the right things.

Luck appreciated my status in the neighborhood. He liked that the old dudes were looking out and that I had my mind focused on sports. Luck chimed in, not allowing me to be on the block for too long, still making sure I was always aware, because anything could happen at any time.

Luck was still trying to find his footing in Baltimore. He just had to figure out what he wanted to focus on, get back in school, and resume his basketball career. I felt it wouldn't be hard, because everybody who knew Luck knew that he was hands down the best guard in Baltimore.

CHAPTER FOURTEEN

ANOTHER BALTIMORE

"Cut that shit off!" my stepdad yelled through my wall. "Is you hard of hearing? Shit!"

The music wasn't even that loud—I think he was just looking for a reason to fuss. Deek really wasn't doing that well. He was battling diabetes, and diabetes was clearly winning. A few days earlier, Duke and I had been sitting on the steps inhaling a pack of Twizzlers. We were talking about football, and we saw Deek stumbling up the block before collapsing in the middle of the street. I leaped off the porch and ran over to him, putting his arm around my shoulder and lifting his heavy body up off the ground.

"Hey, yo, come on, man," I said, dragging him toward the house. "You gonna be okay."

When I got him to the bed, he rolled over. His eyes were bloodshot, his face sticky, crusty, and blank. He snapped, "Go get my insulin! And leave me be!"

I grabbed it and placed everything he needed next to the bed. This wasn't the last time I would have to get him from the street or off the living-room floor and into his bed. It had become a recurring thing.

"What the fuck is wrong with you?" Deek yelled in my direction.

"Have a good day, man," I said, leaving out the front door, heading to school.

I could've yelled back at Deek and told him to get his shit together. I could've told him that he needed to be showing me extra respect, because I was the only one really looking out for him. I could've grabbed him and thrown him all over the house, slamming his head into the floor. But that wasn't me, I'm just not a disrespectful guy. My anger and rage got channeled into sports. Those acts of disrespect from Deek had planted a seed of depression in me, but my friends, school, and Luck helped me bury that seed so deep that I often forgot it existed. I also knew that my mother loved Deek dearly and honestly. I had love for him, too—no matter how badly he treated me.

I also thought diabetes had to be extremely painful. He looked so weak during those days. Before Deek's illness, he was the kind of guy who always had work—a handyman's handyman. Imagine that strong Black man in a rolled-up skully cap, wearing suspenders all year round to hold up his old bootcut jeans, worn over some dingy-looking thermals. The kind of Black man who could fix anything—heating, plumbing, HVAC, collapsing roofs, alternators, transmissions, oil leaks, and squeaky brakes. He could probably build a house from scratch. Deek was that kind of guy, super talented, and could do all of that stuff for cheap. He was strong as an ox, carrying ten bags of groceries at once or hauling a refrigerator up flights of stairs on his back. Now he could barely walk up the street without tumbling over. I understood where a lot of his frustration came from. If something I loved, like basketball or football, was stripped away from me, I would feel the same way.

The tension I felt eased as soon as I exited the house and headed to class. I attended Mount Royal for middle school, a completely different vibe from 125. The classrooms were larger, cleaner, and the school had computers everywhere. Even walking there was a journey that allowed me to ignore the chaos at home. When we first moved to Baltimore, my whole world consisted of four blocks. In those blocks, you would find liquor stores, corner stores, churches, a small market, our schools, and the laundromat. Shopping for clothes pulled us out of those four blocks, but everything else we needed was in the neighborhood, and we didn't have to travel far for much. I had no sense of the world outside until I had to walk to Mount Royal. Venturing to this school was like a long walk to freedom or a trip through a freedom machine. I'd leave my house and start out walking through Murphy Homes and then through McCulloh Homes. I passed all of the tattered and half-completed row houses, and then I'd pass the neighborhood we called the Bottom, right through Murder Mall and past Whitelock, where my mom's church was. Then I'd land at Eutaw Street, which was a different world.

Crossing Eutaw Street was like visiting a different planet, leaving a Black world and walking into something completely strange and foreign. You saw something that you never ever saw in the Murphy Homes community: white people. White people jogging, washing their cars, pushing their kids in strollers, sipping cups of coffee, out on their stoops, reading the newspaper, laughing, joking, and having a great time. White people were some happy motherfuckers. Once I saw an old white lady with white hair wearing a white gown and playing a harp. Like, did I die? Where was I? Well, I was in Bolton Hill, which was then and remains today one of the richest communities in Baltimore city. The neighborhood is made up of beautiful three- and sometimes four-story brick brownstones that overflow with character. There are beautiful parks and amenities for the art students who attended the nearby Maryland Institute College of Art and the many doctors, judges, lawyers, business owners, politicians, and rich professionals who lived in that neighborhood, who would never think of walking through the section of the city I called home. My friends and I loved hitting Bolton Hill every Halloween, because those white people took the holiday very seriously. They had no problem giving away full-sized Snickers bars or Twix or large packs of Starburst—all pink! Who knew you could get packs of Starbursts in all pink? Money was not an object to these people, and honestly, after trick-or-treating there, you didn't even want the little pieces of candy and old church-lady butterscotch and mints they gave you around Murphy Homes.

I played Bolton Hill every Halloween and cleaned up, except the one time Duke, Kenny, and I got robbed. Now, of course, this wasn't in Bolton Hill, but you had to pass Whitelock to get back to Murphy Homes. It was around the time that the Larenz Tate movie *Dead Presidents* had come out. We didn't really have any money for fancy costumes, but Duke had the bright idea of just dressing up like the people in the film who tried to ride the armored car. Bright white face paint, black shirts, black pants, and black skullies—we had all of that, got dressed, and went to work. So we had just finished collecting all of those bags of Bolton Hill full-sized chocolate bars and all, laughing at our success, when we came across a group of dudes in an alley, staring at us with hungry eyes and focused on our full bags. "Don't worry, I know these guys, I hoop with them," I told the group. "I'm just going to say what's up when we get close, and we can keep it moving."

I tensed up, poked out my chest as we got closer to the crowd, and led our trio through the alley. When we got to the end of the alley, it was like thirty dudes behind us and another fifteen in front of us.

"Lil' niggas, kick that fuckin' candy out!" one of the older dudes said as they all closed in on us.

Needless to say, we forked over our bags and got out of there. Luckily, none of us was hurt, and of course, we were right back in Bolton Hill the following year, because they had the best candy. Honestly, a beating would have been worth it if we were allowed to keep our bags.

The people in that neighborhood looked refreshed. They never looked beaten down or drained or weighed down by troubles the way you saw with Black people like Deek. The men Deek's age in that neighborhood looked like they could jog ten miles, play catch with their kids, then win the big account, all while maintaining a healthy smile. These Bolton Hill people looked like they did a fraction of the work the people in my neighborhood did while earning ten times the pay. The people from my block, with their two, three, or four jobs, never had time to do yoga in the park or play Frisbee with their dogs. They had to work, probably for someone else's enrichment. The white experience and the Black experience were so visibly different, and every time I walked across Eutaw Street, I witnessed the exchange of realities. As I grew older, I've come to learn that this was how Baltimore works. Millionaires could live on one side of a street, and the projects could be on the other side. Those two worlds would never cross, never make friends, never acknowledge each other. Everybody was okay with it, especially the rich. This was my introduction to how racism plays out. It was also the first time I got an idea of where some of my stepdad's frustrations came from. No matter how much he worked, he could never live like these people—and now he could barely work at all.

I loved walking through that neighborhood. It gave me a sense of power, a different type of security that I could never have back home. I knew I wasn't rich and didn't have a connection to those people. But just being there allowed me to breathe. I used to take the long way home. I didn't care how late at night it was. I wanted to spend as much time in that Bolton Hill community as possible.

There is a lot to be discussed about our failed school systems, and everybody knows about the rough schools in Baltimore. The poor infrastructure, broken heating and AC systems, lack of supplies, undertrained teachers, and tattered, scribbled-on, destroyed textbooks. With that being said, I have to admit that I got a pretty good education at Mount Royal. It was a good school for me. This was my first time out of the neighborhood for something that didn't have anything to do with sports. I was learning and meeting kids from different parts of the city, kids whose whole world didn't revolve around Myrtle Ave. I enjoyed new perspectives; it was cool. I'm sure all of the Bolton Hill kids probably went to private schools, but there were a lot of kids there from different parts of Baltimore, and their experiences were nothing like mine in Murphy Homes.

My favorite subject was math. I was always fascinated with numbers, how they worked, and what I could do with them. I had an equal amount of love for science and history, especially when some of my teachers would sit around and debate stories about activism in the '60s and '70s. That was the time period when my real dad roamed the streets, organizing, protesting, fighting for change. The things he probably had to go through lived on in those stories.

History lessons on Dr. Martin Luther King Jr., Malcolm X, and the Black Panther Party were interesting to me. As a young Black man, I knew we felt powerless on too many occasions, especially in a classroom. But then we got hit with these stories of how these men who looked like us led so many Black people toward new understandings of race, economics, culture, and class. That knowledge, the endless information, gave me hope and forced me to tap in.

"Ay, yo, school is so boring, man," some of my friends would say.

Nah, I'd think. *School is exactly what we need.*

My computer lab teacher was a young Black woman named Miss Johnson. She was cool, funny, and honestly too fly to be a teacher. Back then, when you thought of teachers, you had the image of granny glasses and brown orthopedic shoes, but Miss Johnson wore the latest everything. I imagined the other teachers wanted to know where she shopped, and I knew the students wanted to know. I just thought she was the best teacher who ever existed, and I wasn't alone. She was smart, she knew her stuff, and you could tell she loved teaching. From the first day I stepped foot in Mount Royal, she was supportive. A real, genuine, good person who made me feel lucky and happy to be a smart kid.

My mother loved Mount Royal as well. She always supported my education. My mom had to work a lot, so she couldn't come to all of my basketball games once I started playing for the school. But she always came to the banquets, and she made sure I went to the sleepovers we used to have at the school and that I was good. That meant the world to me, because I knew she had to take care of me and my stepfather while looking out for Luck, my sister, her new baby, and my brothers in New York. I'll never know how my mother was able to balance all of that. Being so young, I wasn't in a position to help ease her load. But I definitely didn't want to add any more stress.

If that meant getting good grades in school, which was necessary for sports, then I was glad to. It was simple, because Mount Royal was literally the easiest school I ever went to. I also helped out with my stepfather, because my mom deserved that.

CHAPTER FIFTEEN

PAINKILLER

Forties of Old E drunk all the way down to the foamy bottom out front by the curb. Twenty-twos of St. Ides clicking and clacking against each other inside a wastebasket. Empty Colt 45 cans by the bed and a thick malt-liquor stench lingering around his room, his body, his aura. This was Luck. He always had some type of beer or a bottle of hard liquor; it became his oxygen. Don't get me wrong, my cousin was still the best basketball player I knew, still popping up on courts in jeans and heavy boots, sliding defenders all over the place, dropping them even, dunking on dudes twice his size. But now he was a drunk, too. I didn't know what happened in New York. I didn't know what brought him back to Baltimore or even what he was going through once he returned. I just knew he needed liquor to cope. It was his number one painkiller. Maybe we all have painkillers. Mom went to church, Jus turned to knowledge and understanding, Wolf needed to disappear and find his sanity in the places he'd venture to—these were all coping mechanisms. Maybe basketball was mine. If I couldn't hoop, I'd feel just as down as Luck. I used it as my way to escape, and I wished it could still be Luck's way, too.

I'd soon find out that Deek had his own painkillers. Everybody knew Deek was dealing with diabetes. It was a very common illness in my neighborhood. I honestly can't think of one person who didn't have a mom or grandma taking pills for high cholesterol or high blood pressure, or injecting insulin, or getting a toe amputated. One day, I was in the house cleaning up, and I walked into the room where Deek rested.

There were scattered newspapers, soiled work boots, loose tools, and a collection of pills in orange plastic bottles with white caps. They had the instructions across the side, like *one every five hours* or *twice daily with food.*

I hadn't thought anybody was in there, but there was Deek. He was in and out of a deep nod, just like the dope fiends posted on the corner who I'd dribble around on my way to the court. I initially thought it must have been some type of side effect from the insulin. Maybe it made him sleepy, and he was fighting to stay awake. I tried not to make too much noise as I picked up some of his hypodermic needles off the floor. Then I started seeing all types of other stuff, including rubber tubing, a scorched spoon, a lighter, a small empty baggie. This was the kit needed for shooting heroin. Deek was getting high.

The thing that bothered me the most was that my mom and sister had to know. They chose not to tell me, as if I didn't live in this house, as if I wasn't running around in the same streets that Deek bought his drugs from. Why would they think that I didn't need this information?

They always kept these kinds of things from me. They hid behind excuses like "We didn't want you to know, we didn't want to hurt you." I can understand that, but I wish they understood this truth: *what y'all not telling me, I'm experiencing outside.* It'd be better if I learned these things from the people I trusted the most. What they didn't tell me about him I learned from people like Wood and the rest of the dudes who ran the block. All this time, I'd been walking around the house on eggshells, trying to be quiet, making sure all of my things were always put away, avoiding Deek at all costs—while still helping him out every time he called my name, "Carmelo!" If he couldn't get out of bed, I got him. If he needed meds, I'd find them. Plus the rest of his requests: milk, eggs, ice, trips to the store, and all of that. If Mom was at work, I was performing these tasks. I was holding him down, so I felt they should have told me what was going on. If I was old enough to take care of him, I was old enough to know who I was taking care of.

During these times, I thought about my real dad a lot. What would he be like if he were alive? Would we be going through all of this? Deek yelling at me all crazy, seeing my family go through so much pain, that pain becoming a part of me. Maybe my dad would've come to all of my basketball games like the other dads I saw cheering on their kids. Maybe he'd help me to become a better player. Maybe I wouldn't even be in Baltimore. I loved Baltimore, but maybe he would have wanted to stay in New York.

I used to ask my mom questions like "Why you ain't never marry my dad?" I never got an answer, though. That only made me wonder about him more and more. But luckily, when we attended family functions, relatives would give me so many different stories about how amazing he was. How he was funny, smart, strong, a leader and revolutionary, the complete opposite of Deek. My dad was fighting to make Red Hook a better place for Blacks and Latinos, and it's probably the reason I love the civil rights movement so much. If my dad had lived, he could have gone on to become the Puerto Rican Malcolm X or Dr. King. He probably would have written a book on social change and starred in a documentary about the movement to advance Black and Brown people. But we lost him. And now I was here, forever stuck with Deek.

On a brisk fall day, I was out in the street playing catch with Duke. I was telling him to go long when Deek angrily limped past us with a look of terror in his eyes. He took about three steps before just tumbling over. He pulled himself up and continued toward the liquor store. Duke and some other kids were, like, "Go get Mr. Deek! Go get Mr. Deek!"

I'd never leave my stepdad out there like that, regardless of how mean he was. I could never have people just laughing at him. It wasn't hard for me to put my pride to the side and just do what I had to do. I ran over toward him to help, and he snapped, "Get the hell off of me, I'm good!"

He wasn't good, but I was sure he would be after he got what he needed from those dudes on the corner. I went to Luck first, because he was filling that big-brother role due to Jus and Wolf being in New York.

"Deek will be good, Chello," Luck would say, taking a swig of his forty. "Don't worry about all of that. Worry about what you supposed to be worried about, and that's being a little kid, B. Just be a kid."

That was sound advice in a way, but Luck also wasn't good. The drinking had gotten even worse—at first, he always smelled like beer, but now you couldn't even catch him without a bottle. He started coming in at weird hours of the night if he came in at all. During the days, he'd walk up and down Myrtle Ave with a golf club, swinging it in every direction like a crazy person who had lost his meds. At night, he kept a sawed-off shotgun tucked in his jeans or under his coat. He was always on the lookout, head on swivel, intensely staring at people, fishing for conflicts, or trying to catch somebody slipping. Basketball wasn't even a part of his conversation anymore. My basketball journey would come up sometimes, but as for himself, he had other things planned.

I heard he had been going around getting in beefs, fighting with people, probably slapping dudes with that golf club, but we never talked about that. One day, he really scared me, coming in the house all messed up, with a busted face and dried blood all over his clothes. I didn't know how to console him. We didn't do hugs and all of that, so I just asked, "What happened, man?"

"Yo, you don't even wanna know, trust me. But I'm good, though, B," Luck said, smelling like spilled beer. "I'm good. Don't worry about it."

Another time, Luck told me strangely, "Always be patient. Chello, always be patient. You going to get what's meant for you."

I didn't understand what he was talking about, but he continued, "You going to get what's meant. If it's meant for you, you going to get it."

I never knew what I was supposed to be patient for. I didn't know what I wanted to do or be. I looked up to Luck and Wood, but there really were no positive role models in the traditional sense. I had some coaches, but I knew part of their kindness was because of my basketball ability. Kids who couldn't play ball were not treated the same way. They were never invited or celebrated, they were left alone. They were normally the first ones to start using and selling drugs. So what was I supposed to be patiently waiting for? I knew no one was coming to save me. I couldn't imagine somebody sitting me down and telling me how to do the things a man is supposed to know how to do. Everything that I had, or ever learned, came out of firsthand experience. The idea of some older dude coming to me, like, "No, *this* is how you shave, Melo," sounded like a sitcom. I'd never had that. Maybe I saw it on shows like *The Fresh Prince*, but that's just TV. My environment was all about kill or be killed. Luck was the one who had showed me that, so what was he talking about? Why was he telling me about some imaginary way of life and not applying those rules to the way he himself was living?

The rumors about my cousin continued to spread. "Ay, yo, Luck robbed the weed spot" and "Luck shot up that block" and "Luck is going to war with everybody, he ain't showing no love." Before you knew it, it wasn't safe for him to be in Baltimore. He had stirred up so much that he had to go back to Red Hook.

"Chello, I'm gonna get myself together, handle some things, and I'll be back," he told me, just like he had the last time. "Hold it down. I'm going to get what I need in New York, and we'll be back on, baby."

I knew I was going to miss him, but what could I do? He was hardly around as it was. So I kept on doing everything that filled up my time. More games at the Rec, spending more time around Kenny and Duke, and working on my game. I still had to look out for my stepdad, but when I had time off, I made sure that I had some fun, too.

I mentioned before about how when I was younger, my mom used to take us to all of these amazing places in New York—parks, movies, trying interesting new foods, and my favorite thing, which was going to WWF matches. In Baltimore, none of that happened. I'm not sure if it was because my mom had to work more or the city didn't have as many activities as New York. All wasn't lost; we did do a lot of family-oriented things, like huge cookouts and family reunions. Relatives from New York and the South would come to town, or we'd go visit them. But normally, when I wasn't doing family stuff, I just hung out with my friends.

Every Saturday, all of the neighborhoods connected to Murphy Homes would link up and go down to the Inner Harbor. Baltimore Inner

Harbor was always a tourist spot, full of cheesy chain restaurants, the Science Center, the aquarium, and paddle-boat rides. But as kids, that was our spot. We didn't know any better, we were fresh off the block. Every bus from almost every section of the city crossed the Inner Harbor or had a stop nearby, so it became a great place to meet up. We used to roll down there with thirty or forty people—young, old, everybody would come. We had to roll in a pack because you had East Baltimore guys coming from one side and the Cherry Hill dudes from South Baltimore venturing from another—everybody wanted to be downtown. When we rolled down, we honestly were just looking for pizza, some girls, and to laugh and have fun—we were never looking for trouble. But we also weren't going to turn down any.

One of those nights, I found myself standing in Crazy John's, the pizza spot we all met up at. As I went to order my slice, the whole store started to beat on each other. I later heard that the fight started over a stolen slice of pizza, allegedly. I didn't have that information when it was happening, because the rumble had started so quickly. If I had to guess now, I'd say that fight was premeditated, because somebody was always looking for a reason to try somebody else. This didn't happen every week, but I was ready for it to happen every week. For half of the walk getting down there, we bragged about what we were going to do to somebody if they played with us.

So this brawl broke out, and I hit some people, and some people hit me, and the whole thing just turned into a wild melee spilling into the streets. Everybody clashing, every neighborhood for itself. You had to fight for your block, because if people found out you ran or cowered, then you couldn't hang out anymore. No basketball, no chilling on a stoop, no selling candy, no nothing. These were the kinds of survival tactics you picked up being from Baltimore during this time.

This fight got real ugly real quick, but it ended because a guy had run through the crowd with a huge foamy-mouth pit bull that looked like it was starving, had rabies, or both. We saw that dog, and all of us turned into track stars. While we ran off, we all made sure that nobody was left behind, because we were loyal to our 'hood. We protected our block and didn't allow anyone to harm or disrespect us. That's what honor meant to us. Just ordering a slice of pizza, you were still picking up important lessons on the meaning of loyalty.

Loyalty has always been a part of me. It's probably the main reason I can never turn my back on Deek, Luck, my brothers, or anybody, even though they weren't consistently pulling up for me. If I knew why Luck was acting out, drinking, and running wild, I would have held him down and would have been loyal. Just like I held Deek down, even though he treated me like a stranger who didn't belong in the house.

I'm loyal to everybody, because I believe in humanity. But I'm especially loyal to my family and the people I love. I would do anything for them, even if I know they wouldn't do the same for me. That's just how I am, no questions asked.

CHAPTER SIXTEEN

FATHER FIGURE

I was around the Rec playing ball like it was any other day. We did a couple of games of pickup, before I played some one-on-ones with kids who lingered after the pickups, and then I went right back to my house. As I approached, I saw my sister losing it, face covered in sweat, tears flowing everywhere, my mom looking the same way, everybody broken. As I looked around, they came to me. "Deek died."

I can't say I was surprised, because I had been there the whole time and watched his decline. Michelle loved him dearly. She had a different relationship with him from the one I had. She could get away with anything, and she knew it, but she wasn't living in the house. She had her own kid to raise. And he loved her in a way he could never love me, maybe because I really wasn't his blood—and the way he treated me reminded me of that fact daily. I only got the stepdad treatment.

My mom had to work, so a lot of the time I was watching him decline, I was alone. Seeing him go from this strong Black patriarch to a small, beat-down husk of his former self. He literally shrank like wool, right in front of me.

I was sad because my mom and sister were so sad, and maybe part of me was going to miss Deek. He was the only father figure I ever knew. As fucked-up as our relationship was, I can never say he wasn't there. He was always there, and that meant something.

I didn't go to the funeral. It wasn't because I was trying to make some stand or be extra tough. I just didn't like funerals and was blessed enough to have a mom who didn't force me to attend. I told her that I had a football game, and she said, "Please go to your game." My brother Wolf came down along with the rest of my family from New York. I watched them all get into their cars to form that long funeral line. After seeing them pull off, I just went to my game.

I also think that was my mom's special way of protecting me from the trauma that comes with living in a place like Baltimore. In Baltimore, Murphy Homes especially, you are going to have a family member or close friend affected by the drug trade. Even if you never sell or use a drug in your life. Drugs are so prevalent, so important to the economy in poor Black neighborhoods like mine, that we are guaranteed to know somebody who overdosed on drugs. Or was shot to death because of drugs, was kidnapped because of drugs, was locked up for life because of drugs, was disconnected from family because of drugs. You can't escape it, it's inevitable.

I used to go to sleep hopeful, but I woke up every morning, like, *Damn, why do I have to go through this? Did I do something wrong? Am I cursed?* That was my mentality, my constant state. And still, as always, I relied on sports to distract me from everything that was around me. If I played ball and only played ball, so much that I didn't have time to focus on my world, then I would be okay. So I got up every day and went to practice and came home. On a lot of those nights, Wood would be out, sitting by my house smoking a blunt.

"Yo, what's up, have a seat," he'd say.

"Chilling, man," I'd say. "Just got back from practice."

"What you got going on? You nice. You be fuckin' niggas up?"

"I do aight." I'd laugh. "I can beat you."

"Yeah, okay!" Wood would say, giving a jab step like Jordan shooting an imaginary fadeaway. "You don't want this work." We'd laugh.

"If you need something, man, let me know," Wood would always say before continuing down the block.

Over time, Wood and I had developed a friendship. He was teaching me things that helped me understand Luck's behavior a little more.

When the weather broke, our little exchanges moved from the steps to the inside of his car, where I'd sit for hours. We'd still be parked in front of my house, and sometimes I'd be in the passenger seat, and sometimes I sat in the back. He would just give me game, while we peeped the block, seeing who was coming around and going away. Telling me stories about the older guys from Murphy Homes, older gangsters, even older than him. How they moved back in the day, what they left for him, and in turn what his generation was gonna leave for us. In a way, he helped me understand some of the pain I felt. Luck probably was acting out because he didn't see a future for himself past selling drugs and getting killed in the streets. Wood didn't show me a clear path to making it up and out, but he did tell me that if I stayed clear of all the things he did, then maybe I'd have a shot.

During those moments, Wood taught me how to master my surroundings and stay on point. It was similar to what Luck said, but he went deeper. Not just being on the lookout but understanding the danger doesn't always come from strangers or people who just pull up. Sometimes danger is sitting at the table with you sharing a meal. Or on your basketball team. Or lying next to you in bed. Don't just be ready for the surprises, be ready in general.

"Never get too comfortable. As a matter of fact, learn how to get comfortable being uncomfortable."

Even on our own my block, I should always be on point—knowing my surroundings, knowing the cars that come through, knowing what's happening during the day as well as the night, knowing who doesn't belong around here, and just making it a point to be on top of everything. From him I learned that I could avoid a lot of that pain I felt, just by always knowing where I was at, who was going to be there, what was their role—and then imagining what was going to happen as a result. Mentally rehearsing the present and the future—always, always on point. Wood did the same for Duke. He liked to play around with him but always made sure we got what we needed.

I remember being on a corner one hot summer day with Wood and

Duke. Duke walked out of the store with a bottle of Diet Mountain Dew. Wood said, "Ay, yo, let me hit that."

"Cool," Duke replied, twisting off the cap, taking a swig, and handing the bottle over to Wood.

Wood took a sip and screwed up his face. When he realized it was diet, he poured out the entire bottle, crumpled it, tossed it into the gutter, and hit Duke with a hard stiff-arm, like *bam!* "Ain't no soft big niggas allowed to be around here! Big niggas can't be soft, I ain't with that. Drinking this skinny bullshit!" People nowadays will probably look at that as bullying, and it probably was, but they need to understand we were living in a different time. Wood wasn't picking on Duke to be cruel, he was training him how to survive on these streets, how not to attract the wrong attention or invite disrespect that would escalate into conflict. We needed that instruction, just like I needed his stories and jokes and rules. Nothing cures depression or eases emotional pain like sitting on the block and listening to some of the funniest dudes in the world. They probably could have gone on to be big-name comedians, if we'd had examples of big-name comedians coming through our neighborhoods. Duke was funny, Wood was hilarious, and I had jokes, too. In a different world, people might have paid to watch us. I know I would.

At that time, I felt like Wood was the only person who understood what was happening to me. Maybe it was because he lived the life. Maybe it was because he was right there watching me go through it every day. One thing is for certain, he gave me something to look forward to the next day. What that something was would often change—some days it could have been a couple of dollars, other days it was one of his stories from back in the day or just an ear I could vent to without being judged. He did those things for me, and that's all I needed to get to the next day.

CHAPTER SEVENTEEN

UNLUCKY

"Melo, pack a bag," my mom said. It had been a long year, and I was so happy that it was coming to an end. What better way to end it than taking a trip to New York to see my brothers and Luck? I missed all of them immensely.

The ride from Baltimore to New York didn't even feel that long, maybe because I was anxious, excited, and happy to be getting a break. There was so much stuff going on in the neighborhood and at school. I just wanted to eat everything in sight, laugh, and be around my family. We arrived at my brother's house early before everybody came, because my mom, who was the best cook, had to make some dishes. When we walked through the door, Jus was sitting there, like, "Wassup, fam?"

We ran over to give him a hug. The whole family started pulling up quickly. It was a huge surprise; none of us knew that he had been released from prison. For the first time in a minute, I started to feel whole again. I had Wolf here, Jus was home, Michelle was being the life of the party like always, and Luck was looking clean and refreshed, like the time in New York had done him some good.

I caught up with Luck at my brother's, telling them about the neighborhood, my school, my friends, and how I was doing my thing on the basketball court. I had all the New York handles like Luck and could score like Wolf. While being in a different city like Baltimore had been tough, I didn't call fouls, I didn't complain, and I could hold my own. Luck chimed in, talking about the Baltimore bump, how dudes down there did 50 putout instead of 21, how he would have crushed St. Frances if he stayed, and wondering if he should go back. That's all I needed to hear.

"Yo, come back, man, come back to B-more. My mom needs you, I need you, we need you, man. Come on!"

"I don't know, man," Luck responded. He was in a whole different zone. He explained how he was building a life in New York, how he had responsibilities, and that maybe it wasn't the right time to go back to Baltimore. My brothers knew Luck was in the streets, and they agreed that Baltimore would be better for him.

"Come back with me," I continued, my eyes welling up. "We can run that town on the basketball tip. I'm solid, you're solid, we need you down there!"

"Don't do that to me. I'll come back," Luck said. "Yo, let me just go to the Bronx and grab my stuff. I'll be back around midnight. I'm sick of New York right now, anyway. I'm ready for a new start in Baltimore, B."

My heart felt that with joy. I didn't think I was going to get to see Jus, and he was right there. Nobody ever knows when they're going to get to see Wolf, and I was spending time with him. But the icing on the cake was Luck moving back to Baltimore in his right frame of mind. He could focus—we could focus—on our games. All of these thoughts swirled through my head as I waited for Luck to get back. One or two hours went by, and I wasn't sure why, but I got this strange sickly feeling. Maybe you can call it some type of intuition, but it's the feeling you get when something bad happens. The kind where your gut freezes and turns. I knew something wasn't right. And then we got that phone call that nobody wants.

Luck had been shot.

"Is he gonna be okay? Is he good?"

Nobody knew.

My mom started crying hysterically. Michelle looked scared, and both of my brothers looked like they were ready for war. *Luck is as tough as they come*, I thought. *You can't keep him down. Any second, he's going to walk through that door.* That's what I told myself, but that sickly feeling inside my gut, that traveling fear, was saying something completely different.

A few hours later, we found out that Luck was murdered by the building where his baby's mother lived. On his way to grab his belongings for Baltimore, he bumped into the guy she was dealing with. They had some words, but Luck brushed it off. I imagined he was happy to get away from that drama and focus on building a new life in Baltimore. Luck grabbed his things and told everybody that he was moving, promising to send money home for his kid. After he left the apartment and exited the building, he stopped to grab a drink from the bodega. The same dude, his baby's mother's boyfriend, was lingering, still running his mouth—except this time, the guy flashed a pistol, aiming it directly at Luck. Luck lunged at him in an attempt to grab his gun. They tussled, and the guy broke away, still aiming at Luck. Luck ran off, but it was too late. The guy shot him in the back. Luck turned around, got up, charged the guy again, and caught twenty-seven more shots.

He was dead on the scene.

CHAPTER EIGHTEEN

THIS IS HOME

After living in Baltimore for five years, I could honestly say that I was locked into the trenches. I was a part of this city, and this city was a part of me. In this little bit of time, I lost friends, loved ones, and people around my neighborhood I didn't even know. Long lines of funeral cars filled my block monthly. I'm not gonna say that I was used to loss. Death hurts. It always has, and it always will. So I'll say that death happened so much back then that I began to expect it. Expecting it always made it easier.

Deek's death sparked a period of darkness, and I felt like it would never stop. Every day seemed rainy, cloudy, and sticky. Summer was never coming. I was depressed at a time when depression wasn't a topic, at least not in my community. I can't lie, I wanted to go speak to somebody. There were times when I wanted to tell somebody what I was feeling, but I didn't know how. I didn't know what to say. I just wanted to be Melo from Murphy Homes—that's all I really cared about. Even in my own household, I never talked about pain.

I never talked about struggling. Why should I? We all knew we were struggling. We all knew we were dealing with things, but wasn't everybody? Wasn't my neighbor dealing with the same shit I was dealing with? I was struggling, you were struggling. I needed sugar, you needed sugar. We all needed to make ends meet. We all had to do what we had to do. We all had to figure it out on our own. One of the main things that allowed me to cope was that I understood that everybody else in my neighborhood was going through the same things. We were guaranteed pain. Their brothers were being killed, their parents were overdosing, and they were living in darkness, too. We lived in darkness as a community. I would never take joy in anybody else's pain, but the fact that we all went through that pain at the same time, dealing with the same kind of madness, let me know that I wasn't completely alone.

I was determined not to let anybody find out about my depression. So I just took all of that pain and hid it. My brothers told me never to cry, Luck never whined, and Wood didn't play that. These were the rules to my world. I understood them and followed them religiously. Vulnerability was a big no-no in my community, and everybody was always okay with this. I mean, they might walk up to you saying things like "I know what you are going through, I lost my brother," or "They killed my best friend," "My uncle died of drugs." Even as they attempted to hug you, it was hard to get past that uncomfortable feeling of *Why is this person being so nice to me, what do they really want?* The type of trauma we had trained us to think that everybody around, for the most part, only wanted to take and never truly want to help. The trauma told us that those hugs weren't free. The shoulder people offered you to cry on wasn't free. Everything had a price. The only question was, were you willing to pay it or not?

Even though sports had always been my go-to, at times even basketball felt small. In the grand scheme of things, what could basketball mean if the people closest to you continued to die or get locked away, which is like another form of death? Nowadays, everybody's going to therapy, singing about therapy, and making therapy jokes—but that stuff wasn't offered to kids like us back then. Mental health never even came up in the conversation; we just had to deal. Nobody was around saying things like "Yo, Melo, you going to be all right," or "Yo, what's wrong? Holler at me." You just hoped the pain you constantly experienced stayed down deep enough and never came to the surface. Maybe sometimes that pain came out on the court or in a fight, but it never came out in regular conversations that involved healing. Because healing wasn't an option.

My mother used to leave the house at around seven thirty, way before me. And I used to wake up and sometimes just lie there. I used to just stay in bed, staring at the ceiling, never wanting to get up, throwing the ball at the wall, thinking of Deek angrily saying, "Put that damn ball away!" But he couldn't now, because he was gone. And Luck couldn't hear me bounce the ball, invite me to shoot shots, because he was gone, too. So I'd crank my music—the same music I'd play all day long. That was my medicine. I used to like to write rap lyrics all over the wall— DMX, Nas, and Raekwon da Chef. I loved all of their music, but I felt like DMX was my preacher. He fit all of the pain I felt into his first two albums. I had an old Walkman with some earphones, and I always kept them with me, always playing X, all day. That was the only way I could block out the things I didn't want to focus on.

I'd find a clear space on my wall, in between the posters and other things, and I would scribble DMX's scripture:

Damn, was it my fault, somethin' I did

To make a father leave his first kid at seven doin' my first bid?

When I wasn't scribbling raps on a wall, I was drawing, doodling Looney Tunes, pictures of *The Simpsons* and other cartoons, and surrounding them with questions to myself like "Why me?" Sometimes I'd just write a bunch of question marks—question mark after question mark on top of other question marks. I really wanted to know, why me? Why did I have to feel this? Nobody never questioned me about what I wrote. I used to get in trouble for writing on the wall, but nobody ever really asked about *what* I was writing on the wall, and I continued to do it.

In this extremely dark time, I had to search for things that made me smile. Some of my better times included walking from Robert C up to Easterwood with my teammates. The jokes never stopped, and we really got to bond. We had to walk through other people's neighborhoods, which was fun because we knew we were going to get into it. We knew we were going to have to fight, but it was never anything crazy. It was just us playing around and having a good time. Some of the neighborhoods we ventured through were full of guys who played on teams we had to face, and the camaraderie on both sides was beautiful. Those laughs and jokes didn't ease my pain, but they made me forget about it. They allowed me not to deal with it.

My long eighth-grade year was finally coming to an end. On top of dealing with my family losses, I had to figure out what school I was going to attend. If you are an athlete in Baltimore, picking high schools is an extremely tough process. A lot of ballplayers who went to their zone schools didn't get the attention they deserved. Then citywide schools were kind of based on the coach you played rec ball for. It's kind of like an unofficial farm system—which meant you could be a really talented ballplayer, but if your Little League or rec ball coach wasn't affiliated with the high school you chose, then you weren't gonna get any playing time, if you even made the team. Those guys were loyal to the kids they coached. They were tied into their families, they dated their moms, they gave advice on dating and a couple dollars when their kids were low on funds. They were locked in.

Kenny Anderson was already enrolled at Paul Laurence Dunbar, a citywide school. I honestly wanted to go there to ball with him, but would I be able to play? Private school was the best option if you wanted to get into a good college, but who had money for that? Definitely not my family.

CHAPTER NINETEEN

COACHES

Choosing the right high school was going to be all about following the lead of my coaches. This wasn't really that difficult, because I didn't have that many coaches. I always played at Robert C, except for the few times I had to venture off with Bay or Madison.

At Robert C, my coach was Mr. Wise. He ran the Rec like he owned it. You would really think his name and finances were wrapped up in the gym's mortgage. Mr. Wise was the coordinator, event planner, director, strength coach, football coach, basketball coach, handyman, counselor, and anything else you can think of—he did it all.

I loved seeing him pull up. Dude drove a burgundy Isuzu. I guess you could call it a truck. And he looked just like a guy who *would* drive an Isuzu—a light-skinned, extra-curly-haired, old-school-player type. He liked to wear jeans with church shoes, sending all the moms into a frenzy.

Mr. Wise was the one who saw me and was, like, "Okay, I'm getting you together. You ain't about to be around here running crazy, thinking you the boss! No, we ain't doing that with you. Come on, come sign up, you're playing baseball, you're playing football, you're playing basketball!" I listened to him, and he made sure I didn't have any free time, enrolling me in every sport Robert C had to offer. Mr. Wise always had a sport for me to play around the Rec. When he recognized my talent, he was the one who threw me out to the wolves. "Playing with other kids is too easy for you, Carmelo! Time to step it up!" he'd say. Then he'd challenge me to go above and beyond my age group and try my hand against the older kids. After I'd punished all the kids in the older group, Mr. Wise would say, "Nope, still too easy, time to take on the next group!"

He'd preach, "No crying, none of that. They foul you, foul them back! They push you, push them back!" Basically reiterating everything I learned from Luck. You wouldn't think basketball was this physical, but in the '90s, Baltimore rec ball was like the NBA of the '80s. Everybody cracked you like they played for the Pistons.

My football and baseball coach was the same guy, Jim Black. Black taught me the rules of sports. He taught me the importance of teamwork, playing together, and he helped me learn to focus in a strategic way.

You could see Jim coming at you from a mile away. He was as big as two guys, round, wide, and with a mouth full of teeth. That dude knew sports like the back of his hand. Baseball, basketball, football, whatever—if it involved sports, he had the facts, stats, projections, strategies, history, and anything else you needed to know. He was a walking sports encyclopedia, and he got respect for that.

By the time I got to middle school, Mr. Wise put me with Mr. Darrell Corbett at Mount Royal. He pulled me aside one day, looked me in the eye, and said, "Carmelo, you got some real talent, and I can't do nothing else with you. You're going with Corbett. I need you over here with him, so that you can reach all of your potential."

The move didn't bother me, because I knew it was a connection between Robert C and Mount Royal. If I played in big tournaments that Robert C wasn't in, I'd play with Mount Royal. So I already had an idea of who Coach Corbett was. Robert C and Mount Royal would always try to make sure that they weren't in the same tournaments playing at the same time. Mr. Wise also wanted to move me because Robert C didn't have the resources that Mount Royal had. Mount Royal had a bigger program, more kids for me to hone my skills against, opportunities for travel, and way more local attention. The best basketball players for my section at the city represented Mount Royal.

I played with Corbett from sixth grade all the way up until the tenth grade, and I can honestly say that he made me. Mr. Corbett would go on to be the most important coach I ever had.

Mr. Corbett was the guy inside the school and the Rec you didn't want to see walking down the hallway. Because when you did, you knew you were in trouble. And basketball players got it the worst. We had to be perfect, or Corbett would make us pay. If we acted out, all of our teachers would send us to him. He would make us pay in longer practice, extra push-ups, more laps, and what we all hated the most: suicides. We'd be, like, "No, ma'am, not Corbett, I ain't trying to go see him. I'll act right!"

Corbett was the one who taught me the rules of the game and how to see the game in a way my peers didn't understand. As annoying as his long lectures could be, I have to say it was the best basketball education anyone could ever receive. Without him teaching me, I never would have made it. He taught me how to be mentally tough and showed me why that was so important. "Basketball is a mental game, Carmelo! Focus!" Sometimes Corbett would embarrass us by doing things like making us do push-ups in the middle of the game. You missed a rebound, "Drop and give me ten." Really, you would be in the middle of a highly contested game, with players from the other team running by you, and you're on the sidelines doing push-ups while being berated. He was a major disciplinarian like that. Standing over you yelling, cockeyed, with his foggy glasses. That guy was a nut, but he was our nut.

He always made me upset. I didn't understand half the things he was talking about in the moment, because I was so mad at the instructions he'd give. However, everything he said always made sense in the long run. It might be one or two months later, or maybe even a year, and I'd find myself saying, "Damn, Corbett was right." Luck had schooled me early on, but Corbett refined everything, making me into a real ballplayer. It wasn't always sweet; we definitely had our moments. One time, I stormed out of practice after telling him, "Fuck this! Fuck you! I don't need this shit!"

This was during open tryouts. He was putting a traveling team together for the Amateur Athletic Union (AAU). Now, we were trying to get the best kids in the city and the county to form some type of super-team. Remember, I had been playing with this guy since I was ten years old. He was basically like family at this point, which could probably explain some of my frustration.

"Y'all got to try out," Corbett said, walking his new prospects into the gym. "Y'all got to play against each other!"

So everybody was playing extra hard, because of these new kids, people who weren't from the neighborhood. These were superstars in whatever county they emerged from—people who were headed to some of the top high schools, public and private, in the city. All of us were going to war, feeling every hit, push, punch, scratch, and bruise. That gym was smaller than a chicken box, and we knocked each other off all four walls. It was really like *Hunger Games*.

I knew I would be playing against a lot of these kids the next year in high school, so I wanted to show everybody now that I was better than them. I made one mistake, and Corbett told me, out of all people, to run extra laps. "Melo, laps, now, go ahead! Go!" That's when I mumbled, "Fuck you, I don't need this shit."

One of the assistant coaches heard what I'd said and ratted, "He said something slick! He said something slick!" pointing at me. "It was him, it was Melo!"

"Man, fuck you, too!" I said, as I started running the laps. Maybe I was mad at the disrespect and how he was going extra hard on me, trying to single me out. Or maybe I was mad that he brought some county clowns down to take my spot. Either way, I lost it. I felt like no matter how good I was, it would never be enough. Talent is not enough. There's politics, respectability, BS, and too many egos. Egos flooded the gym, and for what? Why did I have to sit around here and deal with these people when I could be on Myrtle Ave with Wood and everybody else who truly cared about me? That's where I was going to end up at, anyway.

"What you say?" Corbett demanded. "Repeat that!"

"Man, you heard me. Fuck him and you!" I said.

"Oh, it's like that?" Corbett said.

I didn't respond. I just put my head down and continued running the laps.

"Okay, I heard you, too!" Corbett continued. "You cut. Get out my gym. This is my gym, this is my team. Get out! You want to be in the streets so bad, go back out in the streets!"

I had taken it too far. I didn't have to curse the dude out. But he had also taken it too far. I wasn't about to beg for my spot in front of a bunch of people I was better than. I was hurt, but I couldn't show it. I grabbed my bag, looked at Kenny, and said, "Yo, I'm out!"

Kenny looked at Corbett and then looked at me and said, "Yo, fuck this shit, we out!"

Kenny was my brother, and we had that type of friendship. He was also in the same position, because Corbett had brought in another guard, too. Not to replace Kenny but to challenge him for his starting position. Again, we've been up under this guy since we were kids, so we both thought it was messed up, disloyal. Loyalty was all we had, and he was playing with that.

Who was Corbett to bring these goofy guys down here? It was one thing if he was just trying to get some height; you need height on a traveling team. But he was really threatening our positions, and we weren't going for that.

Kenny and I were walking back to the neighborhood, trying to figure out what our next move would be. Even though I was frustrated with basketball, I couldn't quit on Kenny. He had taken a stand and left with me, so if he wanted to play for another team, I was down. Out of the blue, we bumped into my man Munch who happened to have a car, so we jumped in and rode with him. He was balling for Mount Royal at this time as well.

"Why y'all not at practice?" Munch asked. "Corbett told me to come up. I'm runnin' with y'all!"

"We quit," I said.

"Oh, well, I'm not going. We out, we all out." Munch laughed.

I honestly wanted to take a break from basketball in general—it didn't seem as fun anymore. But again, I wasn't going to leave Kenny hanging, and Corbett needed to learn a lesson. He had been showing off for those county dudes. I thought he needed a reminder of how good Kenny and I actually were. I should tell you that by this time, Kenny was the toughest guard out of the projects—a pure shooter, crazy handles, and a playmaker. He was so good, and took up so much space, that you could easily forget that he was the smartest guy on the court. Kenny was a problem, a bucket, and could play anywhere.

"I got an idea," I told Kenny. "Let's go play for Cecil, jump on with them, and beat the shit out of Corbett and them clown-ass niggas he picked up."

Kenny was like, "Bet!"

Cecil Kirk, located in East Baltimore, was our biggest rival. Not just the Rec but the whole side of town. Playing with them was the craziest thing we could do at the time—and we did it. Proudly bearing our rivals' jerseys and taking the court against our friends and the guy who had been our coach forever, we beat them like they stole something. I scored every chance I got, and when I wasn't scoring, Kenny was—while both of us talked trash to Corbett the entire game. It was probably one of the best games I ever played in my life, and it felt that way. Corbett was pissed, but he knew he needed us. We normally didn't mind his discipline, but he had taken it too far, so we had to hurt him.

That was only a one-time thing. Eventually, we all went back and played for Corbett, because we were loyal, and he was our guy.

My other coach was Bay, the guy who let me roll with him to the Baltimore–DC game back when I was a little kid. For him, I played in special games like Midnight Madness. I had a friend named Lafonte Johnson who spent some time at Towson Catholic and Dunbar before heading to UNLV. He had a game down at Dome, and he asked Bay if I could play because this college coach was in town and wanted to check me out.

This was the first time I ever had the chance to play in front of a real college coach who could've potentially had interest in me, and surprisingly, Bay said yes. Bay was that kind of dude. He always wanted everybody around him to win, and he never asked for anything or expected anything in return. He had money, was fun, and was always looking out for whoever was around him. I played in the game and did a really good job. When I left the court, Bay handed me a pair of Rockports, which were really popular at the time. They were like two-hundred-dollar boots. He just gave them to me like it was nothing, telling me that he might need me to play again sometime. From that day on, Bay was like a big brother to me. If I needed to get out of the neighborhood, he would come and pick me up. If my uniform pants were too tight, he'd replace them. If I was hungry, he would feed me, all while explaining the inner workings of Baltimore's basketball world. Coaches who only wanted to funnel players to certain schools because they received payoffs by way of cash or free sneakers and other merchandise, ballplayers in the street who should have stuck to playing ball, street dudes who never considered pro ball but were good enough to make it, what all of those dudes did wrong, and how Baltimore could crush your dreams if you let it. He also had me balling everywhere, against some of the top athletes ever to make it out of Baltimore, which took my game up a couple of notches.

Corbett had planted those early seeds in me, but Bay had put me in front of the players, ranging from the success stories to the guys who fell off. He became like a mirror image of Wood. Over in West Baltimore, I was learning from Wood the street knowledge and how to move. And I got a chance to combine that with everything I got from Bay, the East Baltimore guy. Unlike in most cities, the streets in Baltimore matter, regardless of what you do. They are ever-evolving, and it's easy to get lost in them. There are countless stories about basketball guys trying to walk the line — running around with this drug dealer or that drug dealer, carrying a gun to the gym, missing practice to be in the streets, and then trying to score thirty points a game. But you can't do both; it never works. Baltimore is a tough city in which you must survive. You do need to know the rules, but the application of those rules is everything. Witnessing the game and using those rules to weave your way through the game, those are different from playing the game.

   Bay and I remained cool. None of those coaches really tried to push me to go to one high school or another. They left it pretty open, and I kind of felt like I had enough talent to go somewhere and start, so why not hit Dunbar with Kenny? After all, he was my point guard, and the school was free.

CHAPTER TWENTY

TOWSON CATHOLIC

I decided to attend Dunbar, even though at that time the Catholic League in Baltimore was the biggest thing. St. Frances, Towson Catholic, Calvert Hall, Mount Saint Joe, Cardinal Gibbons, and Loyola ran everything. Those were the biggest schools for the top players at that time.

Since it was all about the Catholic League, I always wanted to see if I was up for that challenge. But I'd need a scholarship. I wasn't about to commit to any of those schools if my mother had to come out of pocket and pay anything. She already had enough on her plate taking care of everything after Deek died, so I wouldn't dream of adding another bill. I enrolled at Dunbar High School and was looking forward to playing with Kenny.

Before the Catholic League had taken over as the farm system for potential pros, almost every guy from Baltimore who went on to play in the NBA starred at Dunbar: Muggsy Bogues, the 5'3" sensation from Lafayette Housing Projects; Reggie Lewis, the legendary swingman who was like Scottie Pippen before Pippen; Reggie Williams; NBA champions Sam Cassell and Keith Booth; and David Wingate, too. When Dunbar was winning, which was often, you could hardly get into the gym. The walls would be packed, standing room only, the benches overflowing with screaming fans. Playing for Dunbar was like being a pro on the local level. Dunbar was probably the only public school in the country that attracted scouts from everywhere, all the time. The school had the hype, the alumni, the history, the legacy, and the fans. I didn't think I was going to the NBA; that was the last thing on my mind. However, if I wanted a chance to compete outside of the Catholic League—and to be anything, as far as basketball was concerned—then Dunbar was the school.

Paul Laurence Dunbar High School was named after a famous African American poet. It was originally a "colored school" and only the second school in Baltimore to award diplomas to Black students. Being in Dunbar High School was cool, because I got instant respect. Kenny was already tied in, and everybody knew I played basketball. Dunbar also had a strong history outside of sports. The first Black businessman to build a billion-dollar company was Reginald F. Lewis, not to be confused with NBA player Reggie Lewis—and *both* of those dudes had walked these halls, just like me. Wandering around the school was like a trip through an African American museum; you could feel the history in the building. The walls were lined with pictures and quotes of greats like Harriet Tubman, Malcolm X, Dr. Martin Luther King Jr., and Frederick Douglass. My favorite was the Douglass quote that read, "Once you learn to read, you will be forever free."

Meanwhile, I had also applied to Towson Catholic. I had filled out the financial assistance forms with my mom. Surprisingly, two weeks into high school, we got a phone call telling us—I couldn't believe it, never in my life did I think—I was accepted into the prestigious Towson Catholic. All of the best basketball players from West Baltimore at that time were going to, or wanted to go to, Towson Catholic. And they chose me? I knew I was good, but in a way, getting into that school gave me a validation that I didn't know I was looking for. *I can play with these guys. I can play at this level. And I will.*

I thought I had a full scholarship to Towson Catholic. Years later, I found out that my mom still had to pay. She kept it secret, because she wanted the best for me, and that fancy Catholic school was by far the best. My mom was always that kind of woman. She never had to say how hard she worked or what all she did—she just made a way, and for that

I'll be forever grateful. Dunbar would have been a good school for me to attend but not as good as Towson Catholic, especially as far as sports were concerned. The elite basketball players from West Baltimore, the ones I looked up to and who were already on the roster, were Lafonte Johnson and Keith Jenifer. I wanted to be like them—guys from my neighborhood, going to these big-time Catholic schools and really putting up numbers on their way to being stars. Deep down inside, I knew I was good enough to play on any team. But I didn't say it; I didn't really profess my dreams. I didn't own them myself. But I kept pushing toward them anyway, always thinking about what Luck said: *What's for me will be mine; be patient.* I left Dunbar and prepared to start Towson Catholic the next day.

Towson Catholic was a far cry from Dunbar, to say the least. Dunbar had a lot of Black teachers and administrators, and more than 90 percent of the students were Black. Towson Catholic was the exact opposite. The ethnicity of the student body didn't bother me as much at that time in my life, but it's the little things. For instance, my hair— braids were normal at a school like Dunbar, but they were strange and unacceptable at Towson Catholic. But again, I was honored to be at the school, so I didn't mind taking out my braids and wearing a blowout. I imagine that I probably looked like my dad back in the day, Big Curly with the big curly afro floating up and down the court. The few Black boys at the school with long hair knew the deal, so they had 'fros, too, and the white kids looked at my hair like they wanted to touch it, but they knew better.

Everybody was waiting to see what I was going to accomplish as far as basketball was concerned, or at least I thought so. I'd had a great summer, performed well in every league I was in, and destroyed opponents from every part of the city. I had even beaten dudes who were older than me, and I was only expected to get better. I tried my best to fit in, even though I stuck out like a sore thumb. Being Black and from a neighborhood like Murphy Homes, going to Towson Catholic was instant culture shock. Those students had money, cars, and resources on resources. They came from two-parent households. They'd never been to housing projects. They didn't have stories about dead relatives, the people they saw get shot, or dribbling on bloodstained concrete on the way to the park. I was foreign to them, and I knew this. So I did my work, kept my head down, and played by their rules. But still, even though I tried to keep a low profile and kept my living experiences to myself, I failed out of varsity. My undoing was a confusing, boring, uninteresting theology class that taught lessons about a God I never knew. Basketball players needed a 70 average in every class to play, and I had one 68 in theology.

"Is there anything I can do? Any extra project? Makeup work? I really need to play!" I told my teacher.

She just said, "No."

I asked her over and over again, telling her that I needed the grade to play. She wasn't having it. The craziest thing about the whole situation was that I had never been disruptive in her class. I did have a lot of questions, because how they saw God and how I saw God were different. For them, it was all one-sided: God works like this and that, and if you don't listen, you are headed straight to hell. This was the Towson Catholic model, and if you questioned their interpretations, you were deemed a problem. I wished someone would have told me that going in.

I had been gone from New York for many years, but seeds had been planted during my time there. We were encouraged to be open-minded, to listen, to ask questions, and to be a part of the academic community. Early on, I was taught that true learning came from everybody being able to contribute, not from lectures from an unchallenged authority. Especially with topics as personal as religion, God, good and evil, and life and death. How could a teacher just dictate the great truths and expect us to accept them blindly? To me, this was the most irresponsible thing in the world. I never shut my teacher down or said her ideas were bad. I just didn't get where she was coming from. I honestly wanted to learn more, to gain better understanding. For the first time in my life, that hunger for knowledge—which people like my big brother Jus got praise for and praised me for—worked against me. At Towson Catholic, developing your own opinions and asking questions to better your understanding—those were bad things.

My questions didn't come from left field. My mom was in the church, and I had been in church my whole life. Even though I wasn't forced to go, I had plenty of ideas on God, how God worked, and what God wanted us to do—especially in regard to how we treated other people. The lessons they were teaching me at school weren't adding up. "Well, how come you see the Bible one way and my mom sees it a completely different way?" I would ask questions like these almost every day during my first semester, and that wasn't me being disobedient. It was just, like, "Why am I supposed to accept this information as the be-all and end-all? How is a high school teacher supposed to be recognized as an authority over my mom, who has probably been in church longer? I can't question you?"

And the answer was a hard "No!"

My curiosity got me called into the office for a meeting with the principal and the vice principal. They clearly said, "You can never question what we teach you here. You should never question religion or the manner in which we explain it to you. You can never do that, and you won't do that if you want to stay here!" I tried to tell them about my mom, Sunday dinners, celebratory Easter, community involvement, and the church she attended—they weren't interested.

"You listen to us and us only," the vice principal said. "And that's it! I don't want to hear about you being disruptive anymore. Or you will never touch a basketball at this school!"

Towson Catholic was always heavy on the religion and took it very seriously. It was part of the curriculum in every way—we were always reading the Bible, quoting the Bible, learning to understand the Bible, and being sent to mass. I wasn't fully with it; their methods didn't seem right to me. Religion in the Black community is always rooted in being connected, surviving, and praying for change. There was nothing in

Towson Catholic's lessons about healing. It was a form of control: "If you don't do this, you are going to pay in the worst way, forever!" My friends back home would trip when I told them that I had to study the Bible like homework and go to mass all the time. They would ask, "Yo, what the hell is mass?"

"You go in there. You pray through communion, they give you the shot of juice, a dry little cracker," I'd tell them. They stared at me, confused, laughing. "I'm going there just for the snacks, man. You know I'm always hungry. I will go in there to get that cracker and juice as many times as they would let me!"

The school eventually made me sit down with the priest, the monsignor, and all that. Those old dudes kept talking and talking and talking. They explained mass and what holy communion is, the purpose of this form of worship, and why we must to do this. They were just on me about every single thing. This was by far the craziest school I had ever been to in my life. And the funny thing about it was that I wouldn't be talking about any of this stuff if I couldn't play basketball. I understood communion, just not theirs. My mother's in the church, but her communion was not good enough for them. She didn't do it the way they did it, so they saw her as being wrong. None of that sat right with me.

Towson Catholic did me dirty. I couldn't play varsity my first year. I literally came to that school to play varsity ball, and I couldn't. So I had to play JV, and I can't lie, my ego kicked in. I was crushed. Those guys were terrible, and if I was sitting on a bench next to them, then I felt terrible, too. All of my other friends, the people I played with at Robert C, Mount Royal, Cecil, and everywhere else, were playing varsity. They were mentioned in newspapers, noticed by college scouts, and really doing their thing. I was sitting here on JV, and to make matters worse, I had made a powerful new enemy.

The worst thing that could've happened to me was failing that theology class, because the vice principal put a target on my back that never went away. I'm not going to call him a racist, but he was definitely the guy at the bank who rejects your loan application for reasons he can't disclose. He always had a smirk on his smug face when he looked at me. I got the message: *You're only here because you're Black and can play basketball.*

"Carmelo Anthony, come to my office." I heard this consistently for the remainder of the school year. It was problems with my hair, or my shirt, or any other small thing that he could pick at. After theology, he just hated me. A Black basketball player, having the nerve to question the way in which God was taught at Towson Catholic. I didn't know my place. I needed to be shown how insignificant I was to him, the school, and the world.

There was so much buzz around me attending this school, and I felt like they didn't even want me. Coming in, everybody was talking about me and my man Darnell Hopkins, who was also from the neighborhood. Darnell was like an all-American who was nice in every sport. He was the man. When we were growing up, everybody used to always rave about how he was the best they had ever seen. If we were playing baseball, then he was the pitcher throwing 90-miles-per-hour fastballs like Roger Clemens. If we were playing football, then he was the quarterback slinging 50-yard bombs downfield like Brees, but could also scramble like Vick. On the basketball court, he was the point guard, but he could also score. Darnell had it all.

I always tipped my hat to him. He was definitely the man at Towson Catholic and in Baltimore city sports at that time. He made me feel like I had to work ten times as hard to avoid being lost. His gigantic shadow eclipsed my neighborhood, rec ball, and now my new school. And this extended beyond the court, because he was a good guy: clean-cut, the kind of kid the adults at Towson Catholic loved. Darnell's uniforms were perfect. He always had on the right dress shoes, was always saying, "Yes, ma'am," and "No, sir." Those white people ate it up. *Darnell is so special, he's not like the rest of them.* And by that, they meant me. So I had to always watch what I said, what I did, and how I reacted in certain situations. He was the barometer I was measured against. The definition of how young Black men should act.

"Yo, how they treating you at the school?" Bay would ask on days we worked out or hung around his crib. "You like it?"

"They keep comparing me to that kid Darnell," I'd say. "It's like I'm under a microscope; everything I do has to align with what he does."

"Don't worry about it, they love him because he's producing," Bay would reply. "Just keep playin' hard, your time will come, you'll see."

I was lucky to have somebody like Bay to drop those thoughts and feelings on. I wasn't angry. I was always happy for Darnell; I never hated on anybody. I just knew I had to be aware that they were looking at him. They were expecting all the other Black students, the city kids from the 'hoods and the projects who were only there to play ball, to perform just like him, on and off the court. Without the proper guidance, our confusion could easily turn into anger, and we didn't need that. We needed to present a united front at all times. It is important for Black students to promote unity, especially in white spaces. The last thing I needed was for anybody, especially the people at the school, to think we had a problem that didn't exist. Darnell and I had both entered that school with plans of playing varsity as ninth-graders. He made it easily—unfortunately, I didn't.

That took me out. It made me feel worthless, forcing me back into my shell. I wasn't wanting to connect with anybody, do the schoolwork, or even stay. It's funny how everyone lectured us kids about how important education is, how we need to be educated. But it was only tied to the requirement for playing sports. Kids who didn't play sports were always able to avoid the long education rants, making it all seem so phony. I didn't care about school; I felt it wasn't for me. And maybe if I were on the team, I would have felt differently, but I wasn't. And it took a long time to get to school, like an hour. Then all the white kids would look at me funny, and my teachers were messing with me about my hair, telling me I can't wear this, and I can't wear that, braids were not allowed. And they won. I stopped going to class toward the end of the season, and I stopped going to school, and I gave up on my freshman year, not caring about my grades or that school in general. I was constantly asking myself whether I'd made the wrong choice when I decided to attend that school.

I didn't know what type of vibe I was going to be on. It was frustrating. *I wonder what Luck would do?* Drink a forty of OE to the foamy bottom? I didn't want to do that—I had seen how alcoholism destroyed Luck and what drug abuse did to Deek, so that wasn't an option. But I did need a way to clear my mind and escape the madness. So I chose fun, which led me back to Dunbar, hanging out with Kenny all the time. Together we'd joke so much that I'd forget I was in so much pain. We had seven periods at Towson Catholic, but Dunbar had four periods. By the time my seventh period was over, I was shooting down on the bus or the light rail. I arrived at Dunbar and literally walked right inside the building. I would get there probably by the end of their third period or beginning of the fourth, which was their last period. I would just be down there, hanging around the gym playing ball or eating in the cafeteria.

I played at the school so much I felt like I went there. The principal and teachers paid me no mind; they thought I was another student. I met a couple of friends, had some fun, and honestly thought about transferring. I could have played at Dunbar easily—I knew the team's style, and I know I would have made varsity. I felt I was better than everybody they had in my position and could have probably dropped 20 or more points a game as a sophomore. At Dunbar, I would be All-Metro. As a matter of fact, I would be player of the year, a legend, with the skill set to bring them back to the glory they were known for. The whole idea felt great. *What do I need to do and where do I need to sign to ditch Towson Catholic and their stupid rules?* This conversation danced around in my head for months, on the bus ride to Dunbar, as I shot around in the gym at Robert C, and when I just hung around my block: *Go to Dunbar, Carmelo. At Dunbar you will be king!* But I couldn't do it, I couldn't just run away from those people like that, proving them right. Eventually, I realized that running was the easy way out. Anything I could accomplish at Dunbar I should be able to accomplish at Towson Catholic—if I was as good as I thought I was. I wasn't sure what Luck would do for himself in that situation, but I knew he wouldn't tell me to take the easy way out. After all, Luck took the easy way out when he left St. Frances. I bet if he'd had another chance, he would have stayed. Looking for the easy way out had never worked for me. I had always been better at dealing with all my problems head-on. I decided to stop hanging around Dunbar, go back to Towson Catholic, master their rules, and finish out my year.

One thing I never wanted to be was a person who broke promises. When I found out I had to play JV, I told the coach that I was going to trust the process, work on my game, finish the season, and prepare for next year. Since I'd said it, I had to do it. The varsity coach was always in my ear, saying, "We are going to bring you up. We're going to call you up for the tournaments, so you got to make sure your grades are right."

I didn't really listen to the promises they made—my ego wouldn't allow me to set up another disappointment—but I did what I said I was going to do. I finished the season. Our record was horrible; we went one and fourteen. But I finished.

I was so happy that the season was over. By the summer, I just let it go. I wasn't going to spend my time thinking about playing varsity versus JV. *If I'm going to play, I will play.* I hit the AAU scene and tore everything apart. The high school experience worked wonders for my game, because the bump with upperclassmen made me stronger, listening to the different coaches taught me more about the game, and playing with my friends again gave me a jolt of confidence. I needed to remember who I was, the kid Coach Wise forced to play with older kids. I had more experience and was getting stronger, way stronger, strong enough to bump with older men over the Cage or up the Park. People were watching, and my stock was going up in the city. No national attention, but in Baltimore my name was ringing bells. Leading into my sophomore year, I knew I was going to make varsity. I promised myself that I wouldn't stress over playing time. I just wanted to pass my classes and make sure I was able to do what I had to do.

Later that year, I began experiencing excruciating pain that would linger for a long time—sore back, throbbing and burning arms and knees. People said it was going to happen, people were waiting for it to happen. I wasn't thinking about it happening, but when it happened, it happened.

My mom is 5'9"; that's pretty tall for a woman. My brothers are 6'3" easy. Old Polaroids show my dad's 6'6" frame towering over whoever he stood next to. So when I woke up in the mornings screaming, "Ma, I can't go to school today. Ma, I can't move! My legs hurt. My knees hurt," she knew what was happening.

"Carmelo, you are growing. You need a different bed," she said.

We switched everything, dragging out my thin twin bed, using Michelle's old full-size bed. Bought new sneakers, because my feet were expanding as rapidly as the rest of my body. New khakis for school, because my pants only reached the middle of my shins.

The growth spurt was real. I went from 6'1" to 6'5" or 6'6" in a matter of months. If I hadn't retained the same baby face, people probably wouldn't even have recognized me. But being recognized was the least of my problems. Initially, I couldn't walk, the pain was too much. My body was paralyzed, constantly aching all day and night. It was so bad that taking pain pills would have easily been justified, but I didn't do that, I just endured. When the pain subsided, I lacked coordination. What's even more crazy is that fighting to regain that coordination caused more pain. I'd wake up in tears, wondering when the pain was going to stop. When would walking become normal again?

In the beginning, I walked with a crazy limp. Even if I spent all day lying around the house, my body still felt like I'd played ten games of basketball on cement. After a couple of months, the pain went away. Its replacement was confidence. Something special had happened, and I felt untouchable. Still quick enough to battle guards but big and strong enough to go into the paint. Talented enough to destroy people who were already headed to college, I had arrived. It didn't matter if I was playing rec ball or on the blacktop with older dudes. I was the kid from Murphy Homes who was built like a man and played like a god. For anybody who wanted to go up against me, this was going to be a long summer.

CHAPTER TWENTY-ONE

GAME ON

My first order of business was to follow the rules in a way I hadn't connected with during my freshman year. I decided to never say anything in theology again. I needed the class to pass, and all of these trips to the principal's office just weren't worth it. They blocked my goal. The vice principal and those teachers didn't care about my family history or how I felt about God. They'd made it very clear, so why should I give them my energy? That wasn't going to do anything but prevent me from playing.

I never abandoned my questions, and I still remained a curious kid, but I felt like school was not the place to explore. My mother was a deaconess, and she had her views, and I continued to work on mine as my own personal journey. I'd often wonder things like, *What does God look like? How do you know you chose the right religion? Do we all go to heaven? Is Mom right? Is the school right? Deek was mean as hell—did he get into heaven? Are Muslims right? What about Five Percenters like my brother Jus? Do these white Catholics even know what being a Five Percenter means? Why would God speak to my teachers and not to me?*

I kept my questions to myself and worked really hard to come back— extra homework, staying after school, and everything. I wanted to ball with Darnell. I thought we would be a powerhouse, and we both were looking forward to linking up. That meant doing what I had to do.

You could wear a bush, but you couldn't wear braids. This was the hairstyle I'd worn since I was four or five years old. I didn't fuss, I just respected it and followed the rules. I combed out my braids and wore a neat afro. Anytime I touched my hair or twisted a small piece, I earned a trip to the office, so I tried my best to refrain from touching my own hair. I guess Jesus was down with plowshares but drew the line at cornrows.

There were also no Timberlands—they wanted you to wear narrow Hush Puppies or some other type of church shoes. Keep in mind, to a kid, every minute in church shoes feels like an hour. Eventually, I found some workarounds—instead of wearing the Timbs that look like construction boots, I switched to the hiking Timbs, the ones we called beef-and-broccolis because they were brown and green. Those boots allowed me to follow the rules and still be comfortable. I did all of this because walking into the gym, eyeing that team list, and seeing the name *Carmelo Anthony* in bold letters meant the world to me. This was why I came here, why I took those long bus rides, why I spent so many hours in the gym, why I kept my mouth shut during theology. To be on this list, at this time, representing this team. *I'm doing this*, I repeatedly told myself. *I'm going to shine, and the only person who can prevent it is me.*

I came back after the summer ready to play varsity. I was in the mix, and I just felt like I was going to have a great year. I'd never played better basketball in my life, and I started getting minutes as soon as the season began. My game wasn't all the way there yet, as I was still getting used to the growth spurt. But I started showing people that I was here to stay, and the gossip started. "Y'all see Melo? He's really good, man, he's gonna be a great." I didn't listen to the noise, I just kept playing ball. Then, all of a sudden, our best player on the team, Keith Jenifer, ended up leaving to attend military school. Now the team belonged to me and Darnell. And everybody started asking who would be the leader, was it going to be Melo or Darnell? And again, I didn't listen to the noise; I blocked it out. That became my strategy, to spend more time working than dreaming, more time doing than imagining. And all that hard work paid off, as I felt like I got better with every game I played. People started to try to pit us against each other. We never had any personal beef, but I'm sure he thought he was better than me—same as I thought I was better than him.

Darnell was good—big, strong, and a solid point guard—but I just knew I was better. I don't know why, but I just knew. I guess the problem for me was that a whole lot of people didn't know, and that spiraled into a real debate. I always felt like I had to work extra hard at everything I did. I had to prove it to myself and everybody else. What's even stranger is that I had this determination despite the fact that a few months prior, I had been about to quit. This has always been my relationship with sports—and a response to any type of adversity in general. I go from these extremes of not caring to trying to prove everybody wrong. I can trace this back to different moments in my life, starting with my friend who stole my chain. I regretted that I allowed him to do so and vowed to never let it happen again. I took that loss hard, and I did not like how it felt. The feeling of defeat doesn't sit well with me. That's the reason I fought so hard for my keychain that was stolen when I first moved to Baltimore. It's why I aggressively attacked Luck on the court during our battles, even though everybody knew I was too small to beat him. In the end, people would remember my effort more than my size. I was not going to allow people to place Darnell ahead of me easily. If he ran two sprints, I had to run four sprints. If he did one hundred push-ups, I was right behind him doing two hundred. I was not going to be beaten.

That drive made me a top player. It led to me being named the *Baltimore Sun*'s Metro Player of the Year and Baltimore Catholic League's Player of the Year. I finished that season averaging 14 points, 5 rebounds, 4 assists, and 2 steals. We went 26–3 and finished third in the state tournament.

Darnell was still the starting point guard on the team, and he became one of my closest friends. We went to war together on the court every day that season. He lived in my neighborhood, so we spent a lot of time together commuting and such. None of the drama about who the team belonged to ever came between us. We worked out together, shared meals, dreams, and everything else—Darnell and I became family. We constantly used our competitive edge to push each other forward. It was beautiful, because we were both strong as individuals, but

together, nobody could touch us. We made Towson Catholic the team
to talk about. Darnell and I even played summer ball together that year,
joining a team called Baltimore Blue. Baltimore Blue was put together
to challenge DC Assault, which was one of the best AAU teams in the
region. It was led by a superstar named James White, also known as
Jumping James White because of his ability to dunk from the free-throw
line like Jordan.

White was going into his senior year, and I was a rising junior—but
he was also Maryland's top player and already nationally ranked. Everybody knew about White, he was such a big deal. It was a Baltimore-
versus-DC game, and we played at Towson University, not too far from
my high school. It was only a one-hour car ride away from DC, and
the whole of Baltimore and DC came out, packing the gym from every
angle. I knew that they mainly came to see White, so I had to perform.
I was kinda nervous. I had never matched up with a player as respected
and well known as James White. He was supposed to be the best, the one
everybody thought was everything. As I looked at the crowd, I imagined
that they all wondered who White was going to embarrass, who he would
dunk on. White knew this, which was probably the reason he didn't look
nervous at all on the court. He was jogging up and down, seeming as
though he didn't have a care in the world.

As we got into the game, I got a chance to get a good look at him. I
realized he wasn't as big as I thought he was. We bumped around a little
in the paint, and I learned that he wasn't as strong as they said he was.
But man, that guy could jump. He could fly, even, but I could jump,
too—so that canceled out. White scored, and I scored. And then I scored
again and again. In the process, I realized that this guy could not stop
me. There was clearly nothing he could do to prevent me from putting
the ball in the hole. I wasn't vocal, I didn't trash-talk. I just kept hitting
jumpers, getting to the rack, catching and-ones, and throwing it down. I
ended up dropping, like, 30 points on White in front of his own cheering
section. The whole crowd went wild, because people outside of Murphy
Homes and Mount Royal didn't know I could score like that. I myself

was surprised, because if these moves could work on the great James White, then they could work on anybody. It was the first time I felt like I was the one. I didn't let that one good game go to my head, but in the back of my mind, I knew that my performance had meant something. There were some great players in Baltimore you had to look out for. And now Carmelo Anthony was added to that list.

My whole mentality changed at that moment. I was taller, my body had adjusted, I was stronger. White was a great player but not better than me, not in that moment. If they called him number one, then they should be looking out for me. My Baltimore Blue coach, Joe Connelly, who was also my high school assistant coach, kept putting the battery in my back, like, "Yo, man, fuck these guys. You are better than all of them!"

Joe was an overly energetic, basketball-obsessed white boy everybody loved. He was one of the reasons I was able to function at Towson Catholic. Joe was always there, not just as a coach but as a liaison between me and the school. He was also the best hype man I could ever ask for: "Yo, fuck this guy! James White can't fuck with you!" he kept saying. I was feeling all of that energy, and I was ready to take on whoever.

I remained extremely active for the rest of that summer—locked in, killing everything in the city. It was to the point where people stopped asking about Darnell. They all wanted to know what Carmelo was going to do. It was my team.

CHAPTER TWENTY-TWO

TOO BIG FOR TOWSON

When I came back my junior year, everything clicked. I was already good from a basketball standpoint, and I felt I was in a position to do something really special. I knew I was going to make it to college at this point; I just wanted to make sure I got a full scholarship at a school I loved. Number one on my list was Syracuse, so getting there was my focus. I always loved Syracuse ever since I was a little kid—the players, the color of their jerseys, and how the gym literally shook during big games. Mike Lloyd from Baltimore and other players I knew who attended the school always talked about how they enjoyed their time there.

Bay was good friends with Mike Lloyd and knew a lot of guys on the Syracuse coaching staff. One of them approached him at a game one day and asked about me. He knew Syracuse was one of the schools I always liked, because I talked about the Orange so much.

Joe, my assistant coach, wanted me to go to Maryland. He wasn't trying to force me, but I know that's where he wanted me to go. I liked Joe a lot, but I didn't want to attend that school. I asked Bay for advice, and he told me to follow my heart, do what made me happy, and never try to live for all these other people. Because at the end of the day, I was going to be the one who had to live with my decision.

Bay's involvement in my decision had pissed people off. They started questioning our relationship once colleges started coming around, asking questions like "Why is Bay hanging around Melo so much? He must want something." But I had to shut them down, because Bay was there for me when a lot of people weren't. He had my back when I wasn't ranked or a number one player or this big college recruit. When I was just a kid trying to survive, Bay helped me survive. He gave me an education on how to move in these streets, the kind of education money can't buy, on top of giving me actual money. Everything was always genuine with him—when we couldn't hang, he'd give me a couple of dollars to take whatever girl I was dating at the time to the movies and TGI Friday's for wings. When we could hang, Bay would always come and pick me up. At one point, I was hitting his phone every day, catching basketball games with him, or hanging around his apartment playing video games while his girlfriend cooked us dinner. I truly believe that if I didn't have him, I would have been just hanging around, and something bad could have happened to me. My outings with Bay were transformative. They gave me time to laugh, have fun, learn, and escape the anxiety and depression that came with being expected to be this great player— as well as the traumas I never really healed from, the loss of Luck, the absence of my big brothers.

The pressure that comes with being a big-name athlete, out of nowhere, is immense. I was quickly learning that everybody wanted me to be everything. Everybody instantly attaches their dreams to you, and you have to make it happen. People couldn't even imagine me saying something like "I don't want to play basketball anymore." They were spending my checks before I even got them. And I loved my family, all my friends, and my block, too. I knew I couldn't let them down. But at times, I just really needed to get out of the neighborhood. I needed breaks from the madness.

When Bay and I weren't watching games, he was having me test my skills against some of the best players. On one of those days, Bay took me to this fancy gym in Pikesville. There he and his inner circle held some of the toughest pickup games in the city. It was one of the nicest gyms I ever played in. Some players from the Baltimore Ravens used to work out in there and even played full-court with us sometimes. Even though

I was still in high school and undersized, I could hold my own against those guys. Same with most of the people I had to face up against, until I matched up with Mark Karcher.

Mark was a superstar. He used to be on Luck's team at St. Frances and was now playing at Temple University. His basketball journey was completely different from mine. My fame kind of popped up once I reached high school, but he was the man since he was a small child. There are countless legendary stories of the top college coaches sneaking in to some of the roughest neighborhoods in Baltimore just to get a glimpse of Mark—and he never disappointed. Mark mastered his 6'5" frame. With the finesse of a guard and the footwork of a young Olajuwon, he was the total package, truly unstoppable. Everyone knew that Mark was destined for the NBA.

Of course, they made me stick Mark, and he got the best of me, easily slamming me around, bullying me in the paint, and completely shutting me down. None of my moves worked. There was nothing I could do. I fought and fought, but he was too big and too strong. I felt I had let Bay down. I definitely let myself down. People were telling me not to worry, because I was so young, but I was used to winning. That loss made me work harder.

I kept telling myself that my junior year was going to be the year. I wasn't coming in as a question mark. Everybody knew I could do everything—dribble, pass, shoot, and lock down on defense. And even though I was still bony, I was used to my height. I felt all of my guard skills and fast footwork coming back. I envisioned the season being like a coming-out party for me. All of the superstar seniors were gone, the remaining upperclassmen were admiring my game all summer, and the focus was on me. I was Towson Catholic.

I was extremely focused. I already had the rules down; I knew what I could and could not do and how to toe the line. And in this case, the line meant their strict and obnoxious list of rules. There was no way a guy like me ever considered stepping over the line. I may have been a rebel at heart, but I could save my silly antics for after school, because there was too much at stake. Towson Catholic had begun to get a lot of attention—the school's popularity had grown as quickly as the Carmelo Anthony name, and that angered the vice principal. I think he could have dealt with another kid gaining this type of success, but since I had questioned his religion, wore an afro, and didn't check all the "good Negro" boxes, he was upset. Then, as the year progressed and I got even more attention, his anger intensified. The *Baltimore Sun* wanted to do a story on me, the school, and our big year—and he had a problem. Our local TV news station WBAL, channel 11, wanted to walk the halls with me for a feature about how I'd made it from Murphy Homes to being one of the top basketball players in the state. It was an extremely positive story and a good look for the school—and even so, the vice principal had a problem. Anything that touched on Carmelo Anthony's basketball skills, journey, and potential made him upset. I have never seen an adult have such a grudge against a kid. Not to mention a kid who brought so much positive attention to the school.

But I guess he must have prayed to Mary or gotten some kind of counseling, because his behavior changed suddenly. He stopped trying to punish me for all the little stuff he used to pick on me about. It just went away. This guy went from standing on my neck about everything to giving me my space and completely leaving me alone. Maybe I can give the credit to God. Maybe I can take the credit for myself, because Towson Catholic was the number one or number two basketball school in the state. Maybe I had become too valuable for him to harass. I know that all the praise I got made him upset, because he'd still look at me hatefully as I walked down the hall. He never said anything else to me out loud, but that look said everything. I was good with the silent treatment, because I didn't want to talk to dude anyway. I will say I was bothered at the way he began to reference me. Even though he would never talk to me directly, he would frequently talk about me: "Well, Carmelo is going to do what he is going to do, anyway. He thinks he runs this school."

Then, pretty soon, he stopped referencing me completely, as if I didn't even go to the school at all. The funny part is that by this point, I was doing more for the school than it was doing for me. The popularity I brought to Towson Catholic had stretched far past the administration. It started bothering some of the parents as well. The Catholics didn't like this black kid from the projects of West Baltimore being the face of their school. They were over it. Everybody loved the fact that our team was winning, but this was a Catholic school, a private school, in a racist county. Basketball should not have been the core reason for the media attention. And then the fact that this attention was brought on by a guy with a name that most of them could not pronounce? Strangely, Christian charity never came up in any of these conversations.

The way these people responded to my unexpected success told me everything I needed to know about them. I no longer felt bad about what had happened in that theology class. My mom had been right, and they were all wrong. I was a child on the receiving end of hate from rich adults who were allegedly religious. My mom, who was never rich, always fed the neighborhood and never turned away anybody, even when we had a small apartment in the projects. My mother never hesitated to allow a person in need to stay with us. She didn't have to go to mass or sit through a long sermon or eat a stale cracker to understand these were the right things to do. That was *my* religious education.

I decided to spend the rest of my time at Towson Catholic enjoying my amazing season and treating people right. I knew there was no way in the world for me to get those people to be able to see things from my perspective. Students and fans made this journey easy for me, and I embraced them all. Being ego-driven was never my style. I never wanted anybody around me to feel uncomfortable, and I truly believe that we are rewarded for that.

One of my greatest rewards came on May 29, my birthday, when I committed to Syracuse. I knew they were going to accept me, because they had been recruiting me like crazy, but it wasn't real until I held that acceptance letter in my hand.

My heart froze and then welled up in excitement. I had done it.

Syracuse offered me a full scholarship as their number one recruit, with the promise that I would get to run the show. I wasn't coming through to back up a senior or learn a system behind somebody else. It was my show. Different coaches from Syracuse had been telling me this since they found out that I wanted to attend their college. They came to every game, and agreeing to attend was the easiest decision I had ever made.

The more my star rose, the more teachers would make corny jokes or say a lot of little slick stuff about my work, as if I wasn't getting it done. But I made sure I got it done, because I didn't want them to have anything to talk about.

Randomly, I ended up becoming really close with the theology teacher whose class I failed during my first year. She was supportive of the basketball team and had worked at the school for a long time. As she got to know me, my curiosity, and my humor, she started to understand why I'd had all of those questions. I also learned how to communicate more effectively and state my feelings. I was no longer coming from a place of anger, I was on a quest for deeper understanding. And while I still did not agree with all of her teachings or the overall philosophy of the school, I appreciated where she came from. She had her own influences and experiences that defined her, just like me. She would offer me help when I needed it; she gave me extra time to complete assignments during the season and ended up being one of my biggest allies at the school. And I really needed allies, because by this point, there were so many teachers who sided with the vice principal and wouldn't even talk to me. The vice principal had a way of spreading his hate for me to other teachers, taking time out of his adult day to gossip and demonize me.

Back then, I really couldn't understand his hate and why he picked at me for so long. At times, I even felt something was wrong with me. Now I understand that race was a factor, but it was deeper. That guy knew that I was special, even before I did. He knew that I would go on in life to accomplish great things, things he couldn't dream of. Instead of supporting me so that I could develop into a person who would proudly represent the school, he chose trying to destroy me emotionally, socially, and educationally.

I made so many attempts to bridge our divide. I knew I failed theology class in the beginning. I was slow to learn the rules, but I was all in. I completed my assignments and represented the school in a positive way. I was a model student, just as upstanding as Darnell, so why couldn't he acknowledge and respect my growth? The love of my mom meant the world to me. If she knew that I was at war with an adult at school, it would have upset her. So I said my "hellos" and "good mornings" to him in the hallway, even though he would look away, never speaking back. I'd help out around the school when I wasn't busy with basketball, and he would ignore that, too. The teachers who sided with the vice principal followed suit. When I'd put my hand up to ask questions, they'd say, "Oh, you. What do you want?" Rolling their eyes to the backs of their heads, looking irritated, fishing for other students to call on—and when nobody else raised their hand, they'd land back on me, saying, "What do you want, Carmelo?" in the nastiest way possible. The sad thing was that I wanted to learn and engage, and I wasn't given a chance. I had loved school for most of my life, and Towson Catholic—with its collection of petty teachers and that jealous vice principal—stole that from me.

When I caught up with Keith Jenifer and Lafonte Johnson, they both told me this vice principal had done the same things to them. He'd ignore you at first or maybe pick at you a little. Then, once you got attention for your talent, he'd flip on you and force you out. This was happening to me. I knew I had to leave. This may sound crazy, but my success had become a problem. You would think that a small, private Catholic school would be happy with the attention and money that players like Johnson, Jenifer, and myself brought to them. After all, that was the only reason they had allowed us to attend. But there was a limit on the attention we could receive, because a lot of the paying parents didn't care about basketball, and the vice principal wasn't a fan of the sport. We were allowed to study and play at the school as long as we were well controlled and didn't receive too much attention. Once we got noticed and started popping up in blogs and newspapers, he wanted us out. Doing another year and remaining sane seemed impossible. I had to get out of Towson Catholic.

Leaving the school wasn't that simple, though. The problem was that I had accumulated so many detentions during my first year, before I had all the rules figured out. Mountains of detentions. Detentions because of my tie, because my shirt was a little untucked, which I couldn't help because I kept growing. I had detentions for getting to school five minutes late even though I commuted over an hour every day. I had detentions for asking questions about God, detentions because of my hair and the way it grew, detentions for having so many detentions. If I completed all of those detentions, I wouldn't finish until I was forty. I couldn't win.

I refused to go to all those detentions because it just didn't seem fair. I had tried my best to play by the rules, but I wasn't just going to let these people walk all over me. So they accumulated and continued to accumulate. By the end of the year, everybody was ready for summer break. That's when the vice principal stopped me in the hallway, saying, "I'm holding your report card until you complete those detentions! I'll see you this summer; there's a lot of scrubbing and cleaning needed around here, Carmelo, and I'll be there to watch you do all of it!"

It was funny that this dude suddenly had all of this attitude. Then I began to realize that he was quiet during the season because I brought the school national attention. I boosted ticket sales like crazy; I sold out the gym, with lines around the block. I had so many people wanting to come to Towson Catholic, I imagined the application pool tripled. I finished my junior year averaging 23 points and 10.3 rebounds, but we lost the state title. I was named Baltimore's County Player of the Year, All-Metropolitan Player of the Year, and Baltimore Catholic League Player of the Year. I'd made my mark, and the press started to cool off. The attention had quieted, and now was the time for him to make his move against me.

"Let's set up a schedule, so I can know the number of days over the summer you will need to attend to complete all of your detentions."

"I ain't doing that. It takes me an hour to get up here by bus," I told him.

He didn't care. He said it was the only way I could get my report card and advance to the next grade. Then he made a snide comment about me not being able to play summer ball. If you know anything about basketball, you know that the summer is everything—the camps, AAU tournaments, and the biggest opportunities to be recognized by a big school. He was trying to ruin that for me. But I was already in a good position. Letters from colleges had been pouring in all year long, flooding my mailbox. A bunch of them even went to Duke's house somehow.

"Yo, man, you got Georgetown, Maryland, NC State, UCLA, and a bunch of other schools all up in my mailbox!" Duke laughed. "Everybody want you, boy!"

I didn't need to perform at a camp or in a tournament, because I was set. I had committed to Syracuse. If I'd held out, I could have potentially run into an issue. Having the foresight to make my decision early made it easy for me to ditch Towson Catholic. The vice principal gave me two choices: complete the detentions or be kicked out. I chose the latter, and I was totally fine with it. I'd had a great year, accomplished so much on the court, and I could finally get away from that administration and those parents who demonized me for unfair reasons. I was from a neighborhood where kids my age were being murdered—my friends and family. And these Towson Catholic clowns were mad because I was too tall to tuck in my shirt the way they liked it? Abandoning that school was as easy a decision as signing to Syracuse.

The first thing we had to do was let the coaching staff at Syracuse know that I had left Towson Catholic and I was going to finish high school somewhere else. An assistant coach quickly reached out, telling my mom that I should go out of town to complete high school.

"Carmelo, you should go to Oak Hill!"

I was, like, "Hell no, I ain't going out of town, I ain't going to no Oak

Hill!" I didn't want to leave my friends to go to some faraway country school in Virginia. They probably had a drill sergeant as a coach who made you march while singing the National Anthem or something. I had already spent so much time at a weird Baltimore County high school. This could be the only year that I got to go somewhere normal, like Dunbar, and play ball with my friends and win the championship before hitting Syracuse. Oak Hill was a terrible idea, a place for those who couldn't get the grades or needed an extra year before college. I could get the grades if I had a chance, and I didn't need an extra year.

But the joke was on me. It didn't matter if I wanted to go to Dunbar or Oak Hill or anywhere else—I couldn't get into *any* school, because I didn't have a transcript. Towson Catholic wasn't releasing it until I completed those detentions. My only option was to go to summer school at Frederick Douglass.

CHAPTER TWENTY-THREE

LEAN ON ME

If I could complete the rest of my classes and get my GPA up at Frederick Douglass, I could graduate and go to college. Going to one of the roughest schools in the city during the summer at night was kind of humiliating. All of my friends came out when the sun went down, so I was missing them—not getting to play ball or chase girls. And most city schools didn't have air-conditioning, so that meant I was forced to learn in a hot, piss-smelling school, full of people who didn't want to be there, including me. There were kids in my class who'd been kicked out of school for fighting, stabbing teachers, bringing guns to school, and all these different things. And there I was, sitting there for detentions.

The teacher at the front of the class looked extremely bored. He seemed to have no hope for the students he was being paid to babysit. The girls who sat behind me always did their hair, Monday through Friday—it was like a mini salon in there. Then there was the guy who would just sit on top of his desk for no reason. The teacher had told him to get off so many times that he eventually gave up and looked the other way. Sometimes dope fiends would stagger in through the side door of the school and flag down the dealers in my class. They would leave and go serve them by the bathrooms, while lookouts stayed by the window. Nobody cared. The whole setup was a complete mess. Some of those dudes were just there to hustle. For whatever reason, they didn't want to, or couldn't, sell their drugs on the streets, and the school provided a safe space for them to get money.

I was down on myself, like, *You are better than this, Carmelo, you are headed to college. What are you doing here?* How did I go from one of the top private schools in the state to being in a class with a bunch of people who didn't really care about education? I'm not judging them, but nobody there really made an attempt to study anything. And I had put myself in this position. My mom worked so hard to provide for me, to give me opportunities that she and even my siblings never had, and I'd put myself here?

My mom never planned on staying in Baltimore for a long time. After living in Baltimore for a couple of months after we had first moved here years ago, my mom wanted to leave. In New York, there were more opportunities for a woman like her. Her administration certificate would have equipped her to work at banks all over the city, and banking as an industry didn't really exist the same way in Baltimore. I talked my mom into staying in Baltimore, because I loved Robert C, and I loved sports, and I was in so many different activities. I promised never to get into trouble. She didn't question me or try to sell me on New York, she just took me in her arms and said, "We are going to make this work."

Mom always kept one or two jobs, but I never knew exactly what she did in Baltimore, other than the fact that she always left early and got home late. I knew she worked at the University of Baltimore, and I imagined that she had an office job dealing with financial aid or in the president's office or something like that. After one of those days dealing with my messed-up school situation, I decided to surprise her at work. I took a combination of buses and the Light Rail over to Eutaw Street and walked to UB's campus. After peering into a couple of buildings unsuccessfully, I spotted her standing tall in a blue uniform. I watched her push a trash can from office to office and classroom to classroom. Mom was a janitor. She never lied to me about her profession, I just never asked. And now I was here seeing with my own two eyes the sacrifices she made for me and my family. At that point, I decided that I was going to work even harder. I would make even more sacrifices, just like my mom was doing for me. If she could suck it up and work a job that she was overqualified for to support me, then I could be working ten times harder at everything I did. The first step would be getting through my time at Douglass.

Douglass at night was like that Morgan Freeman movie *Lean on Me*, before Joe Clark came swinging that Louisville Slugger and forcing everybody to be good. Douglass had no Joe Clark, which was easy to see from the flipped-over desks, scattered papers, and busted notebooks littering the floors. I'd sit back and watch as students randomly wandered in and out of the classrooms, instigated fights, and partied from one end of the school to the other. I didn't join in any of that. I just watched, patiently waiting for assignments that never came.

The teacher would mumble, "Another lost soul, another lost cause," when students floated in and out of the classroom. It seemed he knew we all were going to fail and was happy about it. Even though I knew I could come to class late and leave early, I still followed the rules. Seeing my mom work had ignited something inside me. I was going to get through this. I was going to make it to college.

Week in and week out, I learned nothing. After a while, I made some friends and blended in with the rest of the class. We'd be talking, laughing, joking, and just shooting dice. The teacher never cared, as long as we weren't being disruptive. He got paid to show up and leave, and he was great at that. The summer session at Douglass blew by quickly, and I received every credit I needed to advance. Despite all of those pointless obstacles thrown at me by Towson Catholic, I passed.

CHAPTER TWENTY-FOUR

OAK HILL

The good news was I got my transcript; the bad news was that I missed every camp that summer. I had been invited to them all—Nike, Adidas, everything—but couldn't attend. That was a really big disappointment for a lot of people, because in Baltimore, I was All-Metro, All-City, and Player of the Year.

Kenny was telling me that I might as well come and do my last year at Dunbar, and I thought that was a great idea. I had been wanting to play with him ever since we entered high school, and this was our big chance to shock the world. Me and my best friend, showing everybody how great we were.

Kenny and I started planning, having long conversations about how we were going to crush everything in the city. I was ready, six foot seven, handles, bounce, and nobody could check me. I knew I would be Player of the Year again. But then one of the assistant coaches at Syracuse threw a monkey wrench directly into our plans.

"Carmelo, you are too big-time to play at a city school," he said over the phone. "Baltimore is extremely dangerous. We got to get you out of the city."

"Dangerous to who?" I said back. "Look, man, I'm home, I'm good."

"Carmelo, you are going to be leading one of the top college basketball teams in the country. You are going to the NBA, you will be a lottery pick. We can't have you in Baltimore."

My city would go on to record 256 murders that year. The coach kept saying that I would be a target. People would know that I was going to make it, and they'd want a piece of that. I felt that I was protected. I knew my city and how to move. I knew the people I was around had love for me. But I guess this was their way of protecting their investment, so I listened to what they had to say. There comes a point in every athlete's life when you realize that this is a business. Love and friendships matter, but at the end of the day, it is a business. Syracuse had everything riding on me because I was their top recruit, a blue chip player. Signing me had kept them from giving attention to some of the other top players who might have attended the school. I took the scholarship they offered, so I had to show up ready to play—and be good. That was my end of this business deal.

"We want you to go to Oak Hill," the coach said.

"Fuck no! I'm not going to no Oak Hill, are you crazy?" I said, hanging up the phone.

I wanted to stay home in Baltimore. I wanted to go to Dunbar. I didn't care about Oak Hill. The coach called back multiple times, telling my mother that if I wanted to make something of myself, I needed to be out of the city. And I told her these people didn't know me or what I'd been through. After everything I fought through, even to make it this far—like surviving Deek, Luck's murder, becoming a top player, and never getting in any real trouble—how bad could one more year in Baltimore be?

"This may be my only chance to team up with my best friend!" I told her.

Like anyone who had never been away from home for an extended period, my first reaction was "Oak Hill is too far!" I had just missed the whole summer with my friends because of night school, and now you're sending me to a school all the way out in Virginia? Hell no. Everybody was going to be home, on the block, playing rec ball, going to camp, and everything. I might as well have been talking to myself, though. My mom just heard safe, quality education at a boarding school for rich kids, and she was sold. We never really talked about street violence or how my brothers were in and out of the system. We didn't discuss the fear that puts in a mother's heart. But if we'd had those types of conversations, I'm sure she would have opened up about the fear so many Black mothers have for their Black sons.

"You are going," my mother told me. "Of course, I'll miss you, but this is the best thing for you."

That summer, I was able to play in a few leagues after I finished summer school, so all wasn't lost. Kenny and I played for Baltimore Select, and we were headed to Vegas, so I didn't have to think about Oak Hill and the reality of leaving home for that school as much. We got to play ball and just have fun. They wanted just me to come, but I said, "Man, I ain't going unless Kenny can go and play on the team as well!" and Baltimore Select purchased his plane tickets and everything. Funny thing is that they didn't know Kenny was nice, so we went from playing basketball all day to sneaking out of our hotel room at night and rolling up and down the Strip. Bay was out in Vegas, too, catching the games and supporting us. On one of those nights, well, he caught us.

"Get back into your rooms, you got a game tomorrow!" he yelled, sending us back to the hotel. He laughed about it the next day, because he knew we were just two Baltimore kids trying to have fun. I gained more reputation and became more popular during that Vegas trip. It was after facing a kid named Jackie Butler, who was supposed to be the man. Butler was doing all kinds of damage to my team, having his way with us. On a trip down court, Bay yelled to me from the sidelines where the fans watched, "Man, what the fuck are you doing? You've got to step it up!" After that, I dropped like 20 points straight. Clark Francis—one of the guys who did all the sports rankings—began raving about me. He told Bay and everybody else with my team that I was the number one player.

Kenny and I showed out. I led the team to the Final Four of the Adidas Big Time Tournament, averaging 25.2 points a game. That summer, I also played at the USA Basketball Youth Development Festival, where I helped the East Team win the silver medal. That's when I met

LeBron James. James was a super-talented, fully developed kid from Akron who everybody was calling the next Jordan. He and I were the only two to average 24 points per game and shoot 66 percent from the field. We killed the tournament. He was excited to see me play, just as I was excited to learn about him and see what his skill set was like. We had a great time playing together; I felt like I had known LeBron my whole life. That was the start of a lifelong friendship that will never end.

I went back to Baltimore that summer feeling like the man. Everybody had heard about my performance, and my name was ringing bells. I was a force to be reckoned with. Reebok even sent Bay one hundred pairs of sneakers. I couldn't do anything with them because, one, that could have made me ineligible for taking gifts, and, two, Oak Hill was a Jordan school, which meant no Reeboks on campus. We were only allowed to wear, practice in, and play in Air Jordans and Jordan apparel at the school. So Bay being Bay, he gave them away to all the kids in the 'hood who needed sneakers, which felt even better. Acts of kindness like that taught me the power of influence and money. I could remember not having new shoes unless I squeegeed or sold candy. Now I could facilitate one hundred new pairs going to kids who really needed them. Rich people could make changes in ways that poor people couldn't dream of. If I was rich, I told myself, things would be different. The good feeling from giving away all of those free shoes didn't last for long, though. As soon as I got back, I was supposed to be leaving for Oak Hill.

It was all set up. My mother had everything ready for me to go to Oak Hill. I really didn't have a choice. The day I was supposed to leave to go to the boarding school, I hid at Kenny's crib. Nobody knew where I was at. They were all looking for me but would never find me. I knew Kenny wouldn't rat me out. I just needed to stay away long enough to figure out how I could avoid attending this school. As I did with most of my issues, I took it to Wood.

"Yo, they trying to send me to Oak Hill, man. I'm not trying to go to that school," I told him on the block one day. He spun around and looked at me like I was crazy, like I had three heads.

"Get the fuck out of Baltimore!" he told me. "Go! Don't go to school in the city. Get out of here, nigga! Get out of here. We'll be here, you won't miss a thing!"

"But—"

"It's nothing *for* you in Baltimore, Melo. Go!"

Wood wasn't alone. Bay had been saying the same thing: there was nothing here for me but trouble. But how could they say that? If I wasn't in Baltimore, I wouldn't know them. They were older than me, they never left, so why were they so hell-bent on me leaving? I wanted to stay, I wanted to chill with them, they were my family. They were pushing me away, like I couldn't take care of myself.

The next day, Bay parked on my block and saw me as I made my way back home from Kenny's and said, "Yo, Melo, I need you to take a ride with me, man, for real. Pack a bag, we're going to run out of town for a couple of days."

"Okay, bet," I said. "Give me five minutes."

I threw my bag in the trunk, and we were driving. On the Beltway, past trees, past small routes and exits. I fell asleep. I woke up, and we were still driving. I had no idea where we were going. Bay used to always take me to basketball games all over the place. Sometimes we'd just watch, and sometimes he had a jersey waiting for me at the scores table so I could do my thing.

When I woke up, we were on the campus of Oak Hill. I still didn't know what was going on. I didn't even know where I was.

"You start another session of summer school in the a.m., yo," Bay said. "Get some rest, you got a big day tomorrow."

I got out of the car. It was around two in the morning and pitch-black outside. I couldn't see anything. I was really in the country for the first time.

I couldn't really sleep on the first night, the place felt so strange. I didn't know if I could stay in school out there. All the students knew each other, and these kids were weird. They were from different types of families and places I never heard of. At night, they went cow tipping—it was straight out of a movie.

I didn't really get comfortable until I started meeting people on the basketball team. The coach gave us the lay of the land. His wife was looking out for all the basketball players, feeding us home-cooked meals—chicken, collard greens, yams, macaroni and cheese, and buttery biscuits. But that still wasn't enough. The food was good, but I didn't have a connection to any of those people. I was ready to go. After two weeks in Oak Hill, before the school year had even started, I was hitting my moms, like, "Yo, I'm coming home. Please come get me."

So let me explain Oak Hill. There's a girls' side and a boys' side, and you'd better not cross that line. The basketball team had its own dorm and a dorm parent, who was our assistant coach. When people think of Oak Hill, they think of basketball. A lot of great players attended at one point or another, but it's really just an uppity boarding school. I'd see parents dropping off their kids, slamming their bags next to them, and speeding off without goodbyes or giving out hugs or anything. These rich parents wouldn't even put down their cell phones. I knew I was allowed there for the same reason I was allowed to go to Towson Catholic and, eventually, Syracuse: I could hoop. Most of the white kids or kids visiting from different countries were rich. They had parents who wanted them to attend a boarding school for whatever reasons. The Black kids like myself, most of us, anyway, were the best basketball players from whatever place we emerged. If somebody was from Texas, then he probably was the top player in Texas. The same for New York and for me coming out of Baltimore. We all were competitive. Most of us had committed to top schools. We'd accumulated a ridiculous amount of confidence, because we made it to a school like Oak Hill—and we were all homesick.

The team dorm was a nice spot. When you first walked in, you'd see the dorm parent's room, which was off-limits to us. Past that was the living room and eating area, with a television we had to fight over, a phone we had to fight over, a microwave, a Ping-Pong table, and a bunch of seating.

All of our rooms were upstairs. We all had roommates, and mine was a real cool dude named Chadd Moore who ended up going to Cincinnati. I related to him right way, because we had similar backgrounds. He was from the 'hood in Alabama. I had heard of him, and he'd heard of me. He told me all about Alabama and how he ended up at Oak Hill. I did the same, telling him about Red Hook and moving to Baltimore and how our whole basketball scene worked and operated.

After we got used to being on campus, Chadd and I started noticing the rooms of the players who had gotten there a year before us. They knew how to set their rooms up, and we were ready to follow their lead and make our rooms more comfortable, fun, and livable. We rearranged our furniture and plastered basketball and rap posters across the walls. We became popular really quickly. Other people in the dorm were calling our room the party spot, and a few complained about the music. Eventually, they split us up. My new room was better because I was able to sneak a TV in. There were no cell phones or private TVs at Oak Hill, but I had one, which was good because I didn't have to fight over the TV downstairs anymore. Just like at Towson Catholic and night school at Douglass, I did what I had to do.

One thing about Oak Hill was that everybody was signed to a big college. We could all play. So I had to walk into that situation wanting to be better, knowing I was better, and ready to prove points. It would have been fun to come in and feel everybody out, but I was the number one player. Everybody was gunning for that number one spot, so I had to put them in line. I had to show my strength, because some people said I wasn't strong. I had to show my handles, my scoring ability, and I had to separate myself from the pack, right away.

The basketball part came easy, but overall the first month was really tough. I used to call my moms. "Yo, Mom, please come get me. Send me some money so I can catch the bus home, please. I can't do this. This ain't it. Waking up early, bed's got to be made up, they coming in, knocking these doors down, waking you up, I can hardly use the phone."

And she kept telling me that I was going to be okay. Eventually, this turned into her saying, "Please don't call back, I'm not coming to get you, don't call back. You've got to deal with it. You ain't coming back home." She even stopped answering my calls at one point. So I got up every day, threw on my uniform—the khakis and white Polo shirt they made us wear—and did my job. One cool thing about Oak Hill was that it was a Jordan school, so we had the sneakers, uniforms, and basically Michael Jordan everything.

Our basketball season was a great distraction. Once we started playing, I was less homesick, even though Baltimore was experiencing a sports renaissance. The Baltimore Ravens had just won a Super Bowl the year before, and Hasim Rahman was the heavyweight champion of the world after knocking out Lennox Lewis. Hasim was real tight with Wood and always used to hang in the neighborhood. He even opened a clothing store in Mondawmin Mall called Dreamz, and he used to let us hang around the store, giving us free sweatsuits. All of my friends were home, wrapped in the joy that Hasim brought to the 'hood, and I wanted to be there. But Syracuse was real, and I knew I needed to be playing. I'd get back home to my friends, eventually. But for the moment, it was time for me to do what I'd been doing to get better.

Every day, we had to get up at six o'clock in the morning, clean our rooms, and head over to breakfast. They normally served hash browns with eggs, sausages, bagels, coffee, and orange juice. I'm guessing the rule was that everything had to be basic—good but instantly forgettable. Lunch and dinner were equally boring. You would think that a school with so many rich kids would serve Belgian waffles and French toast or gourmet chicken parmigiana and exotic salads, and you'd be wrong. The food at Oak Hill made the chicken boxes and fish platters from the corner stores back home look gourmet. What's worse is that even if you didn't want to eat the food, they still made you attend breakfast, lunch, and dinner.

The classes really weren't that difficult. It was definitely easier than Douglass, which was a joke, and probably more comparable to Towson Catholic. I had a couple of teachers who were cool and gave special attention to athletes, attention I never asked for. And then there were those teachers who weren't really feeling basketball players like that—the same as it is at any school, and I was used to this by now. You just learn how to arrive on time, do your work, and stay out of their way. Athletes don't really get the opportunity to enjoy a romantic educational experience, like spending hours debating controversial ideas and diving passionately into extra reading. We have to be at practice, we have to play—the school expects us to be on the field or on the court ready to go. That's our end of this business deal. Once athletes understand that the classwork is just an extension of the job they have to perform for the school, they can better adjust their expectations for their classroom and overall campus experiences.

The good thing about Oak Hill is that they forced you to stay on campus. It's a real boarding school; you can't go anywhere. Plus, most boarding schools like Oak Hill are surrounded by nothing anyway. Or at least nothing city kids like us wanted to get into. So basketball becomes your job, and you get better at it. At least, I did.

CHAPTER TWENTY-FIVE

CHARLOTTE

Initially, they would never let us off campus. Cross that line, and all hell is going to break loose. But once the season actually started, they loosened up.

The rules went from you could never leave campus to you could leave with your parents if they came and picked you up, or you could go hang out with somebody as long as they didn't live farther than an hour away. As long as you came back on time, you were good. One of my teammates was from Charlotte, North Carolina. He was a smooth guard who could score with ease named Justin Gray, and he used to go home on the weekends. So I started rolling with him.

I was hanging in Charlotte every weekend, in and out of different neighborhoods, meeting new people, and starting to get a feel for the town. This was good for me. I'd call up Wood every day and let him know what I was doing. He loved that I was staying out of Baltimore and spreading my wings, because he thought there was too much stuff going on back in the city. He even sent me a couple of dollars so I wouldn't be flat broke visiting Charlotte. "Have fun down there, enjoy yourself, Melo!" he'd say.

Being in Charlotte taught me that the South was so much different from the East Coast. It was deceptive to me in a way—not the people but how they operated. For instance, you'd see a bunch of people chilling at a house, thinking they're just visiting Grandma or something, not knowing that's the trap house. In Baltimore, underground economies

moved in alleys and project hallways. In the South, they could be slinging drugs and guns out of a Mayberry-type single-family home. Seeing
that confused me, because I didn't know where the trouble was. Part of
surviving in any rough city is always, always, knowing where the trouble
is. Luckily, I had Justin looking out.

At the same time, my man from West Baltimore, Dee Brown, was a
big star at UNC Charlotte. He knew everybody—putting me down with
the high school basketball scene and the college scene and exposing me
to the world of being a respected collegiate athlete. D even took me to
Johnson C. Smith University's homecoming—it was lit. I was hoping
that Syracuse was going to be as fun as this school. I made sure I had as
much fun at Johnson C. Smith as I could, hanging around campus all
weekend, running up in all the parties, having people think I was really
from around there. Doing everything from Friday to Saturday night,
making sure we got back to Oak Hill on time every Sunday.

My coach Steve Smith at Oak Hill was a great guy. He understood
the pressure that we were under and then asked what he could do to
make our time there a little easier. Interacting with Coach and the
players made my time at the school fly by. Coach Smith's office had
become the hangout spot. A lot of days, we were able to skip lunch just
to hang out in Coach's office and watch old game films and tapes of the
ballplayers we admired the most. He explained things to us, pointing out
weaknesses and strengths, helping us get a better understanding of our
own games.

Those talks and that relationship building transferred to the court.
I had some of the biggest games in my high school career at Oak Hill.
We went on to win a bunch of tournaments that year, including the
Les Schwab Invitational against Mater Dei High School from Santa
Ana, California, and the Bluegrass tournament in Kentucky—and I got
MVP in both. Coming into these tournaments, there were some writ-
ers, basketball fans, and probably coaches still questioning my talent,
wondering if I had what it took. This was the first time people saw me
on a national level, playing against the best players and winning the big-

gest tournaments. I made my team proud, proved myself to the world again—and finally, they all started believing. We traveled the country beating everybody, then landing back home in Baltimore, where we had to face, you guessed it, Towson Catholic.

Now I was back home in Baltimore, and this was a big moment for me. Kind of like a homecoming party after having so much success on the road. And I had to go against the school that caused me so many problems. Everybody was coming to this game—Wood, Bay, Kenny, Duke, and, most important, my mom, who had not seen me play since I left. The game was played at Cole Field House at University of Maryland. They had a couple of players who were supposed to be comparable to me. I made a point of having a huge game against them. That school had to pay for what they did to me, so we didn't only beat them, we beat them bad. I kind of felt bad for those dudes I had to destroy, but then again, they should take up that issue with their corny vice principal. I thought beating them would bring me some type of full-circle satisfaction, but I didn't really feel anything—I had grown past them. The whole team, along with the administrators at the school, felt small to me, and I was on to bigger and better things.

Then I got a chance to match up with LeBron during his junior year at St. Vincent–St. Mary. By this time, James was considered the number one player in the country by a whole lot of people, and if it wasn't him, then it was me. There was talk of him coming straight out of high school and going to the NBA—and I should say he already had an NBA body, so it wasn't a surprise. Everywhere you looked, it was either Carmelo Anthony or LeBron James, and now we would be coming face to face. Our game happened to be at the same time as All-Star weekend in Philly. Since our game was in Trenton, New Jersey, which is only about a thirty-minute ride from Philly, people kept joking that we were part of the All-Star festivities. The game would be on ESPN, and this was my first time ever playing on national television.

LeBron had matched up against Oak Hill a year before I got there. He had a good game but lost. He had been a sophomore then, and now he was a junior who wanted revenge. I was excited to match up with him again; rarely do you see two players as young and popular as we were go head-to-head.

The whole of Baltimore packed that gym, joined by a list of celebrities that was out of this world. Even Vince Carter and Kobe Bryant pulled up. Before the game, Bron had gone to wherever Kobe's hotel was to meet him, and Kobe gave him a pair of sneakers. Bron's team was with Adidas, and Kobe was endorsed by Adidas at the time. Bron played in those shoes, and everybody went crazy because they came from Kobe. The whole experience was amazing. James scored 36 points, while I dropped 34 points and grabbed 11 rebounds to lead my team to a 72–66 win.

This was a crazy moment for me—it almost felt surreal. Playing for Oak Hill while matching up against St. Vincent's and having the world as our audience was something that I had never dreamed of. We watched ESPN all the time, but I never really thought about being a hot topic of the conversation. All I heard leading up to that game, everything was all about LeBron versus Melo. I always worked hard on the court, and I thought I was a great player, but this was the stage. This was the next level, and if I hadn't been able to imagine this, what else was in store? Did Luck see this for my future? During these moments, I always thought back to the days running around Red Hook as a little kid or sitting out on Myrtle Ave. Those were my safe spaces, my homes, the only places where people knew the real me. Those places kept me grounded, reminded me where I came from, and challenged me to never let this stuff go to my head.

CHAPTER TWENTY-SIX

UNSTOPPABLE

After that victory against St. Vincent and LeBron, our team's confidence went crazy. We were on track to be national high school champions. We went back to Oak Hill and beat everybody we played by 50 or 60 points, before winning the Nike Showcase in Houston and then the Nike Academy National, where we faced West Chester, Pennsylvania, the number one team in the country, led by future NBA guard Trevor Ariza. This was the most important game to my team, even bigger than the LeBron game, because they were number one. If we beat them, the number one spot was going to us. And you guessed it, we beat them. We beat everyone we played that year except the time we faced Mater Dei out of California.

We all knew that going to play that game was a bad idea. Oak Hill normally didn't go as far as the West Coast to play, at least not when I was there. We flew out there, and unfortunately we had a long and bumpy flight. We were all tired when we got off the plane. This was also my first time in Los Angeles, and I couldn't really afford to get excited, because I had to focus on playing basketball.

We entered the gym, still beat from the plane. Shortly after the tip-off, we found ourselves in a vicious back-and-forth battle. Once they got a lead of around 7 or 8 points, they started holding the ball and being really petty, trying not to play us. I'd never in my life seen a team hold the ball like this. It was almost like we weren't playing basketball anymore, just catch—and their plan worked. They tired us out and managed to pull out a narrow victory. That loss is still one of the worst feelings I have ever had. We had beaten this team badly in a tournament we'd won earlier that year, blowing right past them in snagging the trophy; I had even received tournament MVP. This game was a complete fluke for us. And just when I thought things were bad, a few days later, they got worse.

"Yo, they killed Wood" were the words that came out of the receiver. I stood there, blacking out, just holding the phone. I don't even remember who I was talking to. My chest caved in and then swelled with fear. I was so far away, at Oak Hill, all the way in Mouth of Wilson, Virginia. *This is not true*, I told myself over and over.

I had gotten the call late. The next day, I woke up to the headline *2 Found Slain in Boxer's Vehicle*. Big Hand Wood had been murdered. Oliver Leon McCafferty, which was Wood's government name, and a female acquaintance, Lisa Renee Brown, both twenty-eight, had both been shot in the head while sitting inside Hasim's car. I wanted to throw up. Wood's death made me feel empty, the same emptiness I felt when we lost Luck. Emptiness, darkness, and uncertainty. I called everybody back home, dialing numbers frantically, praying that the papers had gotten it wrong and that it wasn't true. But it was true, and nobody had any answers for me. Hasim even flipped out on the media, because the reporters wanted to talk more about his car being shot than the fact that one of his best friends was murdered. The idea of Wood being shot didn't sit well with me. He was always the person that clowned dudes who always ran to get guns. He challenged you to fight. He was a real fighter, great with his fists. Yet none of that mattered, he still died by a gun. Wood was more than a part of my support system—he was a big brother to me. His murder gutted me. It was like when I lost Luck and, to a lesser degree, when I lost Jus and Wolf by moving to Baltimore. Finally, I had to realize that loss would always be a part of my life.

Before I went to Oak Hill, I hung out with Wood every day. The fun we had together was a big reason I didn't want to go away in the first place. He was the first guy I talked to after a lot of my games. He was the main person who let me know what was happening in the neighborhood. He always encouraged me to stay away from the dumb stuff, like wannabe gangsters or people who sat around all day with no goals, dreams, or ambitions. Outside of Bay, Wood was the main person who made sure I focused on basketball. "Because basketball will get you away from here and get you everything you deserve in life," he would say.

I kept hearing his raspy voice over and over in my head. "Let's run to the Avenue Market real quick, grab a chicken box!" or "Yo, man, you better not be like dude over there, man. Fuck that guy, he's a clown! And don't be running around with shorty like that. He ain't it!" he'd say during our car rides, pointing at people out the window.

"No, we ain't doing that," he would say if I had a bad idea. He would always fall back on "Yo, you got something, you understand? Even though that's my man, that's our man right there, you not going to do what he did. You ain't going to fuck up this opportunity the way that he did. Once you get out of here, get *out* of here."

Every time Wood told me to stay away from somebody in the city, I listened. And something bad always happened to that person he warned me about. Wood was my guide and guardian.

If I hadn't had Wood forcing me to stay at Oak Hill, I probably would have escaped. I probably would have been right back on Myrtle Ave, probably hanging around him. But I couldn't, because he dreamed of me doing more. We talked the day before he was murdered. Wood was headed to Vegas with Hasim, and you know I wanted to go. "Yo, please send me a ticket. I'm tired of this school. I need a break, bro, I'm trying to see Vegas with y'all!" But Wood being Wood, he didn't allow me to roll. And now I'd never see him again. I had never confronted my depression that started with Deek and grew worse with Luck. By this time, I was a one-trick illusionist, seeming to be perfectly okay while hiding all my hurt and fear. My insides were broken into pieces. On the outside, it looked like I was on top of the world. I didn't feel I really had much of a choice. People were always used to me smiling, and they probably couldn't imagine that I was going through hell. And I didn't wanna let anybody down. I kept that smile up even though it was heavy. Behind it, I felt the weight of all my dead friends.

During my senior year, I averaged 21.7 points, 8.1 rebounds, and 4.0 assists. I was named a USA Today All-USA First Team and a Parade First-Team All-American. I was selected to play in the Jordan Brand Classic, scoring a game high of 27 points, and the 2002 McDonald's All-American Game, where I dropped 19 points and won the Sprite Slam Jam dunk contest. The combination of my performances and efforts led to Hoop Scoop ranking me as the nation's number one high school senior in the class of 2002.

Through the deaths, problems at Towson Catholic, and isolation of Oak Hill, I'd finally made it. I maintained that smile. I got my ACT scores and completed high school. I passed all of my classes. Finishing high school and knowing that I would be heading to college felt amazing.

But I wasn't just off to school as a player who was lucky enough to be on a team. I was going in to run the show. If Luck were alive right now, he'd say, "You earned it, Chello!" He'd pull down his Yankees hat, grab me by the shoulders, and tell me I'd better not let up. He'd tell me to keep applying pressure, and I would listen. We would have been a basketball family—like Stephon Marbury and his brothers, who all played college, and his cousin Sebastian Telfair, who made the league, too. Luck would have been in the NBA, and I'd have been on my way. We'd have bought my mom a big house, and Michelle and Jus and Wolf would get houses, too, along with businesses and whatever kinds of cars they wanted. We probably would have ended up playing for the same team, him at the one and me on the wing, unstoppable just like we always were. But he was gone. It was just me left with all the responsibility of keeping the dream alive.

Honestly, the NBA was the last thing on my mind. I really wanted to go to college. My mom wanted me to go as well; that had always been a big dream of hers. She valued education more than anything. The problem was that my great season had a bunch of people saying that

I should go pro immediately, even though I didn't have an NBA-sized body. There were a couple of guys in the NBA who had skipped college and were doing pretty well—like Kobe Bryant and Kevin Garnett. A lot of sportswriters and some coaches thought I had that kind of talent.

Eric Skeeters, the coach that had gotten Luck enrolled at Saint Frances, started coming around more and more. Now, he'd always been around, but he took a bigger interest in my career. Calling me all of the time, saying that we needed to talk, that he had some things we needed to go over—to the point where it started frustrating me. I had love for Skeets. He was always a funny dude and cool to crack jokes with, but I didn't know why he was suddenly pressing me so hard. He was even coming to my graduation, with my mom and Bay. Skeets had driven my mom and a few family members down. Bay had flown into Charlotte, and one of his homeboys, who was also a coach, ended up driving him from the airport to Oak Hill. Bay was planning a tournament the same day as my graduation, and I had agreed to play in it. Skeets didn't know about this. He had planned on driving me back to Baltimore so that we could have this urgent conversation that we so desperately needed to have. What did he want?

Skeets ended up getting my mom to the graduation late. But it was just in time for them to see me get my diploma and walk across stage, and the joy in her smile made everything worth it. I was so proud. Just thinking of the drama I went through made me feel like this day would never come. Wood dying almost took me out. His words and guidance helped me make it through the darkest times. Now I was here, carrying his dreams too. But more than anything, I was proud to be making my mom proud. And that made me so proud that I totally forgot my disappointment about not wearing a suit.

Not that disappointed, because I didn't own a suit. We had to wear uniforms at our school, so whatever uniform I had on that day was what I graduated in, along with an Oak Hill hoodie. I had imagined myself graduating in a sharp suit in front of a large crowd, but that wasn't my reality. I was okay with that. The same tired outfit I had worn to class earlier that morning was what I crossed the stage in—tan khaki pants, white Polo, and Air Jordans—clutching that rolled-up piece of paper I'd fought so hard for.

"Let's all go out and get something to eat!" Skeets said to our group. "Let's celebrate!"

"We gotta game," Bay piped up, looking at my mom. "Is it okay, Miss Mary?"

My mom nodded her head in agreement. She trusted Bay; they had built that type of relationship. Not just because he gave me a couple dollars when I was broke or helped buy my school uniforms but because he was always there before anybody cared who Carmelo was. When he started advising me, helping me out, and showing me the ropes of the basketball world, he made sure it was cool with my mom first, and she appreciated that. When I would do goofy things like try to hang in nightclubs, he would pull me out, letting me know I had no business trying to grow up too fast. Because basketball would take me much farther than a party at a 'hood bar. I imagine she knew that I needed somebody to explain the streets to me in a way a woman couldn't and to show me basketball players who were supposed to be great but who had gotten sucked up in the Baltimore streets. Bay not only knew these people, but he had a front-row seat—from when their stars were rising to the moment they fell off. He would always tell me this guy or that guy used to have the city on lock, and now he was a bum because he didn't understand what he had. Bay was determined to make sure I always knew what I had. In a way, sometimes I felt like Luck was speaking through him.

Skeets looked sick when he found out I wasn't going out to eat, like he'd just lost his best friend. Bay thought his reaction was hilarious and made jokes about it as we blasted to the airport to make our flight. I was surprised because I haven't seen him in a minute, but again, Skeets was my guy, the love was always there.

I was so busy and running around and playing in all of these different tournaments, so many that I lost contact with a lot of people. But that never stopped the constant echos of "Melo, you should go to the NBA!" Even when I was at my buzziest, coaches, other players, and spectators were saying I should go pro, including Skeets. Skeets never pressured me; however, I knew he thought I could perform at that level and may have persuaded me to give it a try and if I did, he knew I might need him there by my side. But I wasn't going to the NBA fresh out of high school. For one, my body wasn't ready, and I can't stress that enough. NBA guys are like gladiators and you have to be ready to bang with them. And second, when I said my mom wanted me to attend college, I meant it—it wasn't just a talking point. I also had my ACT scores for college; Skeets probably didn't know that at the time. Plus I had committed to Syracuse—and I don't break promises.

Everything worked out for Skeets in the long run. He ended up being the head coach at Delaware State. He had an all-Baltimore staff, including my main man Jim Black, who had been my football and baseball coach at Robert C back in the day. So, we all got what was for us.

I didn't get a chance to spend a lot of time at home that summer because of all the tournaments I played in, but I definitely made sure Bay took me back to that Pikesville gym so I could match up with Mark again, the former Temple star who had embarrassed me when I was younger. Before I left, I had to show those guys that I'd grown up some. And I did—hitting bucket after bucket, doing whatever I wanted to do with Mark, basically doing everything that Mark had done to me the first time we matched up. And of course, they doubled and tripled and quadrupled me, with their whole team collapsing on me every play as I filled it up, scoring every time I touched the ball. There really was nothing they could do; it was my show. Mark stopped me by the door as I exited. "Yo, shorty, you gonna be a problem. I can't wait to see what you do with it. Good game!"

CHAPTER TWENTY-SEVEN

COLLEGE BOUND

I was happy to be out of Oak Hill and on my way to Syracuse. Don't get me wrong, I was thankful for my experiences and being able to play at the school. But at the same time, I was away from home, and I felt like I'd missed my last real year of high school. No senior inauguration, no senior farewell, no prom night, no goofy suit shenanigans—just uniforms, a bunch of chores, nasty food, and relentless basketball. Syracuse was going to be my return to some sort of normalcy. I wished I'd had time to catch up with my friends over the summer, but AAU basketball and training consumed my days, and everything was moving so fast. Duke was figuring out his post-high-school plans, while Kenny had gotten accepted into Maine Central and would be balling up there. So I felt like this was going to be a new world for me. But just as I'd adjusted to Baltimore and Oak Hill, I knew I'd adapt to Syracuse just fine.

I didn't know at the time because I wasn't on campus yet, but I truly believe that Oak Hill prepared me for Syracuse. Oak Hill had the best high school players in the country. The competition, the tough practices, and the hype that comes from being around so much talent at the same time erased any fears that a kid would normally have entering Division I basketball. I knew my peers at Syracuse were going to be really good, but so were my Oak Hill teammates.

I was going in as the number one player in the country, and I do believe my time at Oak Hill pushed me to be in such a high position. I never let that number one player stuff go to my head, though. People were talking, and the papers were dropping articles, but I just stayed close and only listened to my family and my friends back home. In front of them, I didn't have to walk around like I was this big-shot number one player. I just got to relax, cool out, and be Melo. The city of Baltimore knew I was good. The kids who were on the come-up at Robert C, my mom, my siblings, Bay—they all believed in me. As long as I knew I had that, I stayed grounded. There was no space for that number one stuff to turn me into a person I wasn't.

Bay spent a lot of time telling me how fans and haters tore Baltimore athletes apart. They'd praise them when they did well but just as quickly call them clowns when they fell off. I saw Baltimore basketball players who went from being top recruits to corner boys slinging nickel bags of smack. How crazy does it look to be, like, 6'7" on the corner pushing product? Or they ended up working on trash trucks or hanging around the Rec, talking about how good they were back in the day. A lot of times, their downfalls weren't even their own fault. They just had bad advice from people who were trying to use them, not holding them accountable when they made mistakes, and treating them like gods instead of people. I was determined not to have that happen to me. The higher you allow people to lift you up when you are winning, the harder your fall will be. Seeing how some of these guys lived made it easy for me to just focus on being the best player I could be and taking it game by game.

When I first signed with Syracuse, a bunch of random people were out there saying things like "Why you going to Syracuse? They only play zone! Why do you want to be there? They don't produce pros!" I would ignore them, and they'd continue. "Yo, you should be going to a bigger school or something! Don't you want to be a pro?"

Now, remember, these kinds of comments always came from people who were not going pro themselves. I had no idea how they'd become such experts on my life, but they felt they had the authority to critique me harshly. I remember a random stranger pulled up a chair next to me at a TGIF. I had been minding my business and watching a game.

He blurted, "Why you pick Syracuse? Why not Carolina? Why not the ACC? Really, I want to know, I need to know!"

By this time, I'd learned how to ignore these guys, but I decided to answer anyway. I told him, "I want to go somewhere where it's mine, where I can create something. They never won it before. If I play well, along with my teammates, then who knows? We could be the first to do it."

The guy stared back at me in disbelief. Being true to yourself looks to a lot of people like losing your mind. Syracuse was the best decision for me. They had been supporting me since my days at Towson Catholic. I'm a loyal guy, so once I said yes to Syracuse, I wasn't committing to another team. A lot of people make the mistake of thinking that I was making decisions based on a potential NBA career at this particular time. I wasn't. I could have gone to the NBA straight out of high school, but I didn't—that wasn't my goal. I really wanted to go to college. I really wanted to play for Syracuse. Being a pro was the last thing on my mind. I didn't care what anybody said, because I wasn't playing for them. I was playing for me, I was playing for Murphy Homes, I was playing for Wood—and I was playing for Luck.

CHAPTER TWENTY-EIGHT

NEW KID AT SYRACUSE

The first couple of weeks at Syracuse were challenging. I wasn't used to college life, and the whole environment was completely strange to me. I imagine my peers were going through the same thing. The campus was so big and spread out, and you had to take the school shuttle or buses to get to class. You had to figure out where everything was, with nobody to show you. You just had some confusing guides and a bunch of maps. But I made it work.

I didn't quite know what I wanted to study. I definitely loved photography, so even though I didn't pick a major, I minored in that. I loved pictures, images, and trying to capture them. I thought I could maybe be a Jamel Shabazz or even Gordon Parks type with the camera. I might capture images of the people from my neighborhood doing the things that they do—shooting dice, scraping frozen cups, getting their hair braided, slap boxing, double Dutch, tossing jacks, or just hanging out. I didn't know of any street photographers in Baltimore. Maybe I could go back after college and be the first one from my generation.

My teammates were cool. From the start, I tried my best to learn them as they learned me. People probably thought that I would come in arrogant, because I was the number one player, but that wasn't the case. Being the number one player wasn't written in my bio, and it did not dominate my personality. I just wanted to have fun, work out, and play ball. I wasn't coming to take over. I was happy to be there and be a part of what they had already started working on.

The first teammate I connected with was Josh Pace. He had a spot off campus with Andrew Kouwe. They were sophomores and had a three-bedroom apartment. Kouwe also had a car, which made everything seem so easy for them. Kouwe drove a couple of upperclassmen to their classes, and they hooked us up. They already knew the lay of the land, where to party and chill, where to shop, and where everything in the city was at. I was happy to hang around them. Since I was the new kid coming in, I couldn't ask for rides to class or to the mall or anything like that. But I would just hang out and pick up little pointers about life in Syracuse. When they spoke, I paid attention. They made college life seem really fun and were great role models for a kid like me.

At this point, I was still catching the bus everywhere. I was looking like a deer in the headlights, an awkward six-foot-seven deer. Just lost in the sauce without many friends, because I didn't really get to know anyone personally on the team yet. I didn't really have an agenda outside of mastering my schedule. I spent most of my time by myself, just thinking about home. There were some cool kids I met at the earlier orientations, but once classes started, I never saw them again. I was kind of worried. I was hoping and praying that the whole year would not be like this.

One thing about being from Baltimore is that you were always forced to adapt. The worst things happened all the time, and you dealt with them, and you never had a choice. Options are a luxury the poor can't afford. That mentality made being alone start to feel normal. I had been alone when I first got to Towson Catholic. I was alone at Douglass and alone at Oak Hill initially. I didn't mind being a loner; I had played this game before, and I'd always been okay. I would fill my time up by going to the store, the gym, movies, and even restaurants alone. People from the team would look at me crazy, like, "What the fuck are you doing here? Who are you with?"

"I'm by myself," I'd reply. I was happy with that.

One thing about my life is that I always had to learn how to get comfortable in the most uncomfortable situations. That was a survival skill; it was beyond necessary. If I didn't adapt, then that loneliness would have eaten at me. Instead, I rode the wave until I found my community. And I was drawn to what I knew best, the streets.

My roommate Billy Edelin was a smooth guard from the DC area. He was already tied into the Syracuse community outside of the school. He knew some guys from the small projects right next to our campus called Pioneer Homes. He even let them hang around our room sometimes. Billy and I connected because he had gone to Oak Hill. He was a nut, always making DC and Baltimore comparisons, which we'd laugh about. I started meeting those guys through Billy and continued to roll with them when he wasn't around. Billy was like my brother Wolf in a way, a real "Where's Waldo?" type. He was here today, gone tomorrow, and you never knew where he disappeared to. Billy would disappear for days, and I used to go out to the neighborhoods to find him, saying, "Yo, you gotta come back, they looking for you!"

So I started hitting Pioneer with Billy's friends, who became my friends during Billy's frequent absences. They introduced me to a little flea market where I could buy spray-painted T-shirts, socks, underwear, hats, and things like that. I also used to play pickup ball with those guys, hang out, talk trash, and learn about the city of Syracuse. Meantime, I would tell them about Baltimore and how we got down. Of course, they asked about TV's *The Wire*, and I'd have fun telling them that it was shot in my neighborhood, based on my neighborhood, about the people who were from my neighborhood. I even had to walk past that couch from season one; it was in the middle of the projects on my way to school every day. I started becoming comfortable down at Pioneer. I would go after class, before practice, walk around, go mess with the people in the projects, and catch game from the older cats.

Over time, Pioneer became my second home. After a while, I stopped hanging on campus altogether. I'd found a home and a family over at Pioneer, and that was good for me. That lasted all the way up to when the season started.

CHAPTER TWENTY-NINE

BASKETBALL SEASON

I'd gotten a good feel for my teammates from the start, because we'd had the chance to practice and run ball during open gym. Then, once the season started, everything shifted to basketball. More people were checking for the team, finding out about my background and my time at Oak Hill and how I was ranked. Suddenly, my name blew up like crazy, and everybody started showing me extra love. They were always referring to me as the Big Freshman on Campus—the hotshot, the superstar, the one who could take us all the way.

The excitement continued to build. Beyond the school, people from the community started hearing about my skill set. Whispers about me and about the team were spreading rapidly. Being from the bottom, I never forgot that anything you loved or got too happy about could be snatched away in a second. I never allowed myself to buy into all of this new love. Don't get me wrong, the Syracuse energy is real. Seeing that orange everywhere, everybody united in praise of your team, delivers a feeling that can't be conveyed with words. I just knew that I'd had the same unimaginable joy when Luck said he was moving back to Baltimore. Then it was taken in an instant. *Keep your head down, Carmelo. Play hard and stay out of the way, one game at a time,* I constantly told myself throughout the most magical year of my basketball life.

Needless to say, I was never lonely on campus again. We flipped the whole school upside down, winning games, getting invited to every party, special shoutouts from professors, alumni, and administrators.

This was the closest I ever felt to royalty in my young life. I went from being the dude trying to find his way on the bus to being the big dog, the most popular guy on campus.

I used my platform to bring everybody together. I never liked to see people being picked on or bullied. If everybody was calling a person a nerd, I would invite that nerd to the best parties and make sure they had a great time. I didn't care if you identified as a gangster, a youth pastor, or the best hooper on campus, I was going to do my best to connect everybody. I wasn't leaving anyone lonely, slighted, or left out. This was college. We were already stressed-out, because most of our family and friends were thousands of miles away. So everybody deserved to have a good time, to joke around, and to enjoy themselves—and I played my role in making that happen.

From that point on, people started knowing me as Melo who always smiled, who always was happy, and who always wanted everyone else to be happy. This was how I fought my depression. I chose to be grateful, happy, and content with my surroundings—and to constantly bring joy to whoever was in my presence. Being Black and from Baltimore, or places like Baltimore, you and your people dealt with so much loss, more loss than any other group. We couldn't afford to take life for granted; we had to enjoy these moments. If not for ourselves, then for the people who would never get a chance. Luck and Wood would have run around crazy on this campus, lost in the fun. So for them, I had to turn up.

I stayed locked in with Murphy Homes. My basketball success had caught national attention, but I never let it distract me from what was happening on and around Myrtle Avenue. We had those Nextel chirps at the time—and I'd *bloop-bloop* my boys on the walkie-talkie feature all day, checking on them, making sure they were good. They would come to my games, check on me, and join in the fun I was having on campus.

While I was at Syracuse, my big brother Wolf had moved down to Baltimore. I was so happy that he would be close to my mom and sister, because they worried about him a lot. And now I would get to see him in a way that I couldn't when he was in New York, because my mom and sister would make sure he didn't wander off too much. In Baltimore, Wolf would be close to family; they could look out for him. And the best part about me being in New York was that I got to reunite with Jus. He was out of prison, happy, coming to my games, and being that big brother I'd always needed.

Jus would drive to all of my Syracuse games, and if we were playing in Connecticut, then he'd be right there—supporting me, making sure I was good. When I had breaks, I'd hit New York to kick it with him. He'd take me to Delancey Street and buy me Avirex leathers and Pelle Pelle Soda Club jackets. We made up for so much lost time, and I developed a different kind of peace. Jus was heavy into the religious ideology of the Five-Percent Nation of Gods and Earths, and he proudly passed those lessons down to me.

All of the serious dudes from Jus's generation back in New York were Five Percenters. The religion was founded by Clarence Smith, who was more properly known as Clarence 13X or Allah the Father to his followers. His philosophy was rooted in the idea that 5 percent of people were the teachers who knew that God is the son of man. You could reach the level of a Five Percenter when you truly obtained knowledge of self. Eighty-five percent of the population was lost, confused, and enslaved to their closed minds and limited thoughts. The remaining 10 percent represented the rich devils who manipulated us and lied to us about who and what God really is: the original people of the earth, the Asiatic Blackman. There was so much information to consume. Understanding my brother and why he was so tied into these ideas made me want to learn more. As a Black man, I've often felt demonized by these rich institutions full of people like my vice principal from Towson Catholic. My brother taught me that I was doing everything I was supposed to do—being myself, loving my family and where I came from. And the vice principal was also doing what he was supposed to do, as a member of the deceptive 10 percent.

Initially, Clarence 13X was a student of Malcolm X, but he left the Nation of Islam to build his religion and further expand on his own beliefs and ideologies. He believed that Black men were Gods, and Black women were referred to as Earths. He had developed a sophisticated numerology called Supreme Mathematics. Each number held a meaning. For example, if the date was the 26th, then the 2 represents wisdom and the 6 represents equality, which would make the day's mathematics "Wisdom Equality." Supreme Mathematics coincided with 120 lessons explaining 13X's teachings. Jus taught me the mathematics and the lessons, because the only way you can learn is from another Five Percenter. As we made our way throughout New York, Jus introduced me to so many Five Percenters. These legendary street dudes and famous rappers would just come up to my brother and start breaking down the mathematics. It was amazing, making me feel like I was a part of something that was bigger than me. I absorbed it all.

Having my brother back gave me a confidence that I wasn't looking for but that I seriously needed. We became closer than we had ever been, and I enjoyed introducing Jus to the basketball world. He had spent so much time teaching me about knowledge of self, and now I got the opportunity to teach him about the world I was dominating. With Jus by my side, I felt unstoppable. The only thing I was missing was a car. And ironically, I owned one back in Baltimore.

It was a green '98 Chrysler Concord, nicknamed the Green Hornet. I loved that car, with its bald tires and makeshift CD player (composed of one of those tape-shaped adaptors that you slip into the deck while wired to your own portable CD player). Bumping music that way was awkward at first, but you learned to love it, or at least I did. I had grabbed the car at auction before the semester started and left it in Baltimore. I didn't realize that I was going to need it in Syracuse, because everything was far apart. So I had the bright idea of sliding home during Christmas break and driving the Green Hornet back to campus.

We had just played Georgetown. I had a really great game, so good that they wrote about me with my picture in USA Today. That game was followed by four days off, so I left DC and headed straight home to Baltimore to spend the holiday with my mom, sister, and brothers. We had a great time like always, but then I had to roll because we had another game coming up.

"They are calling for a lot of snow, Carmelo," my mom said. "Are you sure you want to drive in all of that?"

"I'll be fine," I told her.

Of course, my mom was right. Moms are always right, but I was young, I had gas on my chest, which means I really wanted to drive, and I was ready to ride out. If I'd come outside to find my car with no wheels, I'd still try to drive that thing back to Syracuse.

It snows in Baltimore; I'm used to that. But it *snows* snows in Syracuse—unmeasurable, ridiculous, offensive amounts of snow. You could get thirty inches and the teachers still wouldn't cancel class. Those are the kinds of crazy storms they're used to. I drove right into the center of one of those storms, and I didn't even make it to Syracuse. I hit a roadblock in Scranton, Pennsylvania.

I drove through the blizzard as my bald tires slipped and skidded around hills and mountains. I cranked my makeshift CD, which was plugged into the tape deck, a contraption I bought from Best Buy, playing the Nas and AZ track from the *Doe or Die* album that went, "Mo' money, mo' murder, mo' homicide," on repeat, only taking a break to listen to the local station so I could gather some information on the storm. I couldn't really find anything until my radio went, "Warning, warning, warning, warning!" A voice warned that driving was prohibited.

There was a huge line of cars pulled over, because the road ahead was blocked. I sat there as long as I could, listening to that "Mo' money, mo' murder, mo' homicide." For a while, the lyrics helped me forget how cold it was and how I was stuck, and I stayed there until I couldn't sit anymore. Luckily, they lifted the roadblock, and I drove until I couldn't drive anymore. I begged my car not to fail me as I made my way to the closest hotel. I was forgetting that I was flat broke and did not have a dollar to my name.

The hotel was several miles away from the exit, but I made it. *Maybe I can just sleep in the car until this storm lets up*, I thought. I tried to fall asleep, but it was too cold. I walked inside the hotel toward a thirtyish, mechanic-looking white dude at the front desk. I was extremely honest, telling him that I didn't have any money, but I would greatly appreciate it if he'd let me just hang in the business center until the storm died down.

"I would love to help you, man, but I can't let you stay in the business center all night," the clerk said. "And all of our rooms are booked."

Running out of options, I asked, "Can I use the bathroom?"

"Yeah, sure."

So I went to the bathroom, and I was just thinking, trying to figure out my next move. I realized that my only option was to be extremely nice, and maybe something good would happen. I walked out of the restroom and approached the front desk.

"Man, there's nothing we can do. Rooms are all booked. I'm sorry," he said before I could even make my case.

This was my karma. I knew I should not have been driving in all that snow. I also didn't have a driver's license, only a learner's permit. I had known it was a bad idea, my mom said it was a bad idea, and I just should have listened.

"I'm a good kid, man. I go to Syracuse. I'm just trying to get to school."

"I'm sure you are," he said. "We just can't do it. But you can sit in here for an hour or so, warm up, and then you gotta go. I can't have you sleeping in the hallway."

The guy walked down the hall, and I was just sitting there wondering what to do. Then I saw a copy of that USA *Today* article sitting on his desk. As he approached, I stood up and pointed to the newspaper.

"Yo, look. I swear to God, man. This is me. That's me, right there in the paper."

The guy picked up the paper and examined it closely. He looked at it and looked at me, then back at the paper.

"Please, man, let me just get a room for the night."

"You know what, man? I'm going to let you stay. But you got to be out of here at sunup, because these rooms are accounted for. I don't want my manager to find out," he said, tossing me a set of keys. I imagined he was surprised because of all the stories that talk about college ballplayers receiving wheelbarrows of cash, and here I was flat broke, not a penny to my name. He could tell, so he looked out, and I was beyond thankful.

I beat the sunrise the next morning, keeping my word. I blasted out of that hotel, out of Scranton, and back to campus. At school, having the Green Hornet made everything so easy. I could get to class, ride around through Pioneer Homes, hit New York to kick it with Jus, and go to the mall whenever I wanted. I was free.

College life was great. I just played basketball and went to parties, in a place where people loved me for playing basketball and partying. This was how you got treated when you won games at a big university. As we prepared for the tournament, even some of my rec ball friends from Baltimore were coming up to Syracuse to hang with me.

I finished the season averaging a double-double, 22.2 points and 10 rebounds. We had been winning games all year, but this meant nothing to my critics. No matter how well I performed or how many games my young team dominated, the critics always gave us disrespect. They'd say things like "They don't have an identity" or "Melo is a freshman, he can't lead a team." There was something about me they just didn't like. It also felt like they were banking on our team not succeeding. I could understand why they thought we were too young or didn't stand out enough, but what I didn't understand was the way they ignored our play, our energy, our confidence, and how we lit shit up every time we got on the court.

Some of them even said that we didn't match up well with the University of Texas in the Final Four. I responded by dropping 33, which set an NCAA tournament record for most points by a freshman. Then I went ahead and followed up in the championship game against the

University of Kansas, putting up a double-double with 20 points and 10 boards, leading my team to a victory.

I, Carmelo Anthony, a kid from Murphy Homes, got the Orangemen their first-ever NCAA tournament championship. I led the team in scoring, rebounding, minutes played, field goals made, and free throws made and attempted. Never in a million years would I have thought that this was going to be my life. I even won the tournament's Most Outstanding Player award. I don't think I needed the validation—I always thought I was a great player—but it still felt so good when it happened. It felt even better when we proved wrong all of those alleged experts time and time again. They ate their words as we cut down the nets and waved our trophies high above our heads.

That year, I was All-Big East First Team and was the consensus selection for the Big East Conference Freshman of the Year, as well as unanimous selection for the Big East All-Rookie Team.

The same people who doubted me all year had become my biggest fans. I ended the season projected to be a top five pick in the 2003 NBA draft. The funny thing about it is that I didn't even want to go to the NBA. This college rush was everything to me, and I planned on staying in school.

We had a pep rally after our big victory. I sat onstage next to my coach, Jim Boeheim, who had just described me as "By far, the best player in college basketball. It wasn't even close. Nobody was even close to him last year in college basketball. That's the bottom line." I was still in disbelief because all of this was just happening so fast. As we addressed the media and fans, a chant broke out: "One more year! Stay one more year! One more year! Stay one more year!"

We'd just won it, and you couldn't tell me nothing. You couldn't tell my team nothing. You couldn't tell my school nothing, because Syracuse just won the national championship. We shocked the nation, and the fans felt all that emotion, and it showed on their faces as they chanted, "One more year! Stay one more year!"

A little choked-up, I addressed the crowd. "I thought you supposed to stay at school for four years. Why y'all keep saying *one* more year?"

The whole room went crazy. People were crying, hugging, and celebrating—it felt almost spiritual. And I meant every word I said. I wasn't ready to go to the NBA, I was just getting used to college. In my heart, I wanted to stay at Syracuse, and I planned to do so. Later that week, Coach called a meeting with me.

I arrived at his office excited. I thought we were going to have a conversation about the plan for next season—who was coming in and how we were going to repeat our success.

"What you want to do?" he asked, closing the door behind me and taking his seat.

"What you mean?" I replied. "I'll be back. Let's run it back!"

"If you don't get the fuck off my campus, it will be the biggest mistake of your life!" Coach Boeheim breathed. "I better not see you on this campus again! You better get out of here! Pack your shit and get out of here."

Coach made it clear, he wasn't joking. I was done. And just like that, my Syracuse career was over.

I knew people were expecting me to declare for the NBA draft; I wasn't completely naive to what my neighborhood and all the spectators wanted. I guessed they were getting their way. Coach figured we had accomplished what he'd set out to do with me. It was time for me to take my game to the next level, making space for someone else. I imagine he thought another season would be too risky, and maybe he was right. In this industry, popped hamstrings and cracked kneecaps can keep poor kids from making millions. Imagine dangling unimaginable wealth in front of a person coming from poverty and then making it disappear because of a single injury. I saw that happen way too many times, and I didn't want that to be my story. I didn't want to see myself getting out of a cab, walking back into my mom's house on Myrtle Ave with a cane and a broken heart, lying to kids, like, "I stayed in school instead of going pro, and I am proud of my decision." As though colleges disappear! I could always go back to school. Some people enroll in their first classes at the age of eighty. But the NBA ain't promised, and it waits for no man.

So I publicly ended my college career. I declared for the 2003 NBA draft.

CHAPTER THIRTY

GONE PRO

I didn't run off campus immediately. I wanted to hang around and enjoy all those championship festivities. Parties on parties on parties, we celebrated for months straight. We ran every club and bar in the whole town. Everybody took care of us. The lacrosse team was winning as well, and I was introduced to frat life, which was too much for me. Those dudes partied at a whole different level. Thinking about frat parties still gives me a headache.

Eventually, I had to slow down, because it was time to train. Laughing and joking and running around campus was for students. I was headed to the NBA, which is not a place for kids. Some big names had entered in the draft that year, like my close friend and high school phenom LeBron James, Chris Bosh from Georgia Tech, Dwyane Wade from Marquette, and Josh Howard from Wake Forest.

Scouts from different teams were sending me to different places to work out with different people and train almost every day. I spent my nights relaxing and prepping for who I had to face, work out with, or train with the next day. After a couple of months of training, the NBA lottery had rolled around. It was time to see who was getting the top pick. The NBA had created the lottery system to keep championship teams from dominating. The system allows the teams with the worst records to get the chance to select potential superstars, in the hopes of saving a struggling franchise. The Orlando Magic have won the lottery back-to-back years—drafting Shaquille O'Neal and Anfernee "Penny"

Hardaway—good fortune that would take that team from being the worst in the NBA to playoff contenders in just a few years. They even made it all the way to the finals. Bay and I watched the lottery back in Baltimore, wondering if we could figure out who would take me. Remember, they were calling me a top five pick. We figured the first team that needed a player with my skill set would be where I'd be moving to.

We watched the television as the Ping-Pong balls with NBA team logos bounced and danced around. Cleveland secured the number one pick. We knew this was a dream come true for the Cavs. LeBron is from Akron, and this would be like a big homecoming party, as it's only an hour away from Cleveland. Detroit won the number two pick. I already knew that they had interest in me, so I started imagining Detroit as my new home. LeBron gave me a phone call, and I congratulated him, because everybody in the world knew he was going to Cleveland. He congratulated me, and we joked about how Detroit and Cleveland were neighbors and in the same conference, so we were going to have some serious fun off the court and some serious battles on the court.

The Pistons had a playoff game against the 76ers, so Bay and I decided to ride up to Philly to check it out. I got a chance to go into the locker room after the game and meet Larry Brown, who was coaching Philly at the time but was secretly set to take the job at Detroit the following year. I'd never heard of anything like that, but I was really excited to meet Larry Brown—and he seemed excited to meet me, too. Shaking my hand firmly, he looked me in the eye and said, "We are taking you with the number two pick, you have my word. You are the best, it's a no-brainer. I can't wait to work with you!"

Shortly after I met Brown, Detroit started sending merchandise: jerseys, shirts, sneakers, and an NBA basketball, so I could get comfortable using it. They even sent me a velour tracksuit with the Pistons logo. My family was planning on where we should live, and the whole situation just felt beautiful.

I was locked in—watching film, training extra hard, and preparing to be a Piston. And then I started hearing about Detroit's interest in this kid named Darko Miličić. I asked around, and nobody knew who he was, but apparently Detroit had their eye on him and they were working him out. I started second-guessing myself, wondering why they'd be working him out. Was there something wrong with me? Did they hear something? We started calling people on the phone, trying to find out where he was so that I could work out with him. I wanted to see what he had. But Detroit was being really secretive; they didn't want anybody to know that they were considering another person. Brown and the Pistons kept moving him around, hiding him from everybody. No one saw him play. I later found out he was from Serbia, and he was also projected to be a top five pick. I still thought Detroit was going to go with me. After all, I came into Syracuse as a top recruit, I led my team to the championship, I had made history. But most important, Larry Brown had looked me in the eye and made a promise. I'm big on loyalty. It matters to me. Above all, a man should always be loyal.

The 2003 NBA draft was held at Madison Square Garden. It was a beautiful sight, so many cameras, so many people, so many monitors. Everybody was smiling, knowing that after tonight, generations of poverty would end for so many of their families. Lanky, eight-foot-tall Black dudes were all over the place. My whole family was there with me. Jus and Wolf even wore hard-bottoms, and I had never seen them in church shoes before. The way their faces glowed made me even prouder. As the ceremony started and everybody began taking their seats, I had bumped into LeBron. He checked out my threads as I checked out his. We both wore the same kind of Steve Harvey suit; his was a cream version, and I had a gray version. We all had the long blazers and bootcut dress pants that enveloped our shoes. I had a quick flashback of our tiny high school frames clashing in camp and reflected on the long journey that had led to us being on this stage together.

The show started. David Stern took the podium and said what everybody in that arena knew was coming: "With the number one pick in the NBA draft, the Cleveland Cavaliers select LeBron James from St. Vincent–St. Mary high school in Akron, Ohio."

I looked at Bron and said, "Yo, let's go!"

The crowd cheered as James prepared to make his way to the podium. He looked at me and said, "You are next!" I gave him a pound as he walked over to receive his Cavs hat and took that legendary picture with the commissioner while holding his jersey up.

There were a couple of minutes between picks. As I waited, I got a call from my agent, who said, "Yo, Detroit taking Darko Miličić."

"What? I got my family, mom, sister, brothers here! They all think that we going to Detroit! They taking Darko Miličić? What happened?"

I was hurt. I was literally hurt at that moment. I was, like, *Damn, would Larry Brown lie right to my face? Could he just lie straight to you like that? Did he get overruled? Why did he flip? There's no repercussions or nothing? Is something wrong with me? Is Darko really that much better than me? And if so, then why has nobody seen this guy? Brown wouldn't do that, he's too good of a guy. I bet my agent is tripping right now. I bet I'm going to Detroit.*

"With the number two pick in the NBA draft," Stern announced, "Detroit Pistons select Darko Miličić!" He said some more words, but for me, everything went black.

My heart dropped. My mind ventured back to my days as a kid. Luck and me, or me and Kenny, or just me, pounding my Spalding on the pavement, inventing new crossovers, imitating Wolf, representing Murphy Homes on the way to the court to practice more moves and perfect my jay. I was always on the front line, ten toes down, as I bobbed and weaved across the cement. All around were multicolored vial caps and cracked-up hypodermic needles. Carrying the pain of my mother and Deek's anger. A world of uncertainty on my back, every time I checked the ball up. Games went to 16. The rims had no nets, and if you so much as thought about calling a foul, you'd get your ass beat. I liked that, because I didn't need any handouts. It wasn't any elite gyms, trainers, or diets. I was raised on candy. I watched dope dealers serve fiends as both groups lined the sides of the court, watching the show. And they *all* used to be nice back in the day. Until they got hurt, got hated on, or never got that shot. Now they just broke days judging my skills, critiquing me, while my opponents and I beat the blood out of each other for their approval. That's West Baltimore.

West Baltimore is a place where the top ballplayers have as many street stories as sports stories. It's not unusual to see lanky lottery picks like me or thick-necked NFL-ready teens huddled up deep in conversation about who got shot, who's snitching, and who's getting money. We adapted to be like that, because even though we were ranked in sports, we still felt like we might not ever make it out. Being a top athlete in Baltimore won't save you like it does in most places. Some of our top prospects were gunned down before they got a chance to show out in an NFL stadium or shake David Stern's hand.

For a Baltimore kid like me, making it to the NBA meant you had to be one of the top 453 players in the world. That was out of roughly 541,000 high school athletes, 166,000 AAU ballers, and 32,000 college players in America. Change those figures into millions if we consider the entire world. On top of those odds, you have to reach that level of success all while trying not to be murdered. I didn't just dribble around bigger defenders and tougher players. I had to weave around poverty, addiction, gunplay, and unresolved pain. I had to beat my past and the traumas that afflicted my family. Compared to climbing out of Red Hook and Baltimore alive, basketball was easy. But I did it; I was there. Without handouts or sob stories or a famous dad. It was just me, my family, and my people. Brown could choose whoever he wanted. By being there, I had beaten more than what any of these coaches could imagine. *I made it*, I breathed, *I belong here.*

Stern approached the podium. "With the number three pick in the 2003 NBA draft, the Denver Nuggets select Carmelo Anthony from Syracuse University."

My chest froze, and the crowd went nuts. I saw them screaming, but I couldn't hear them, as I made the long walk from my seat to the stage.

I smiled as I approached Stern. I firmly shook his hand and pulled my Nuggets hat over top of my braids. *I'm here, Luck. We did it. Let the story begin.*

ACKNOWLEDGMENTS

To all of those who raised me and lived these stories with me. To my mother, Mary Anthony; brothers, Robert and Wilford Anthony; and my sister, Michelle Anthony, rest in power. To Robert (Bay) Frazier, Tynell (Munch) Dunkley, Kenny Minor, and Dontaye Draper. To all those who helped me memorialize these stories—D. Watkins, the publishing team at Simon & Schuster, Asani Swann, Traci Gage, Stephanie Jones, Jaclyn Reilly, and Kristi Yess.